Southern Living.

BEST-LOVED
CHRISTMAS
CLASSICS

Southern Living®

BEST-LOVED
CHRISTMAS
CLASSICS

*Favorite holiday recipes and
easy decorating ideas*

Oxmoor House®

CONTENTS

Celebrate a Very Southern Christmas

When you think of Christmas, what comes to mind? Sitting at the children's table with all your cousins enjoying seconds of your grandmother's best dessert. Or it could be decorating the tree with your family while a warm pot of soup on the stove awaits once the star is placed atop the tree. Perhaps it's the thought of celebrating the season over appetizers and beverages with a group of close friends—a basket of wrapped goodies ready by the front door to be handed to departing guests.

Whatever your memories of this magical time of year may be, *Southern Living* can help you pull it all together with ease and style. Start the season with the Deck the Table chapter on page 9 where several Southern event planners share their secrets to setting a chic Southern table. Next, set a plan for a great holiday gathering with our Merry Starters chapter on page 23 where you'll find updated twists on your favorite Southern appetizers and cocktails. Get inspiration for a memorable holiday dinner with some of our all-time favorite main dishes on page 99 or show-stealing sides on page 63. And be sure to complete your holiday meal with one of our decadent desserts on page 140.

One of the greatest gifts during this busy whirlwind season can actually be time. And *Southern Living* gives you this in abundance with our *Plan-Ahead* tips sprinkled throughout the chapters. In addition, *Wrap it Up* ideas will highlight recipes that work particularly well for quick and festive presents for friends, neighbors, and family.

Thank you for letting us share the holidays with you.

With warm wishes for a merry season,

Susan

Susan Ray
EDITOR

DECK *the* TABLE

Set the tone for your holiday gathering with a chic Southern table. Take your cues from five event planners, who prove that a great holiday fête is all in the details.

CHRISTMAS EVE COCKTAILS

For Gatsby, a great event is all about the theme. When cofounders Kimi Dallman and Glen Collins came on the Dallas party scene in August 2010, they set themselves apart from the crowd because of their event-branding philosophy. "We help create a comprehensive vision for a party and then execute the invitations and various materials that will set the mood," says Kimi. The whimsical-glam Christmas Eve cocktail party seen here is based around the childhood excitement that comes with that day. "We drew inspiration from our treasured memories of Christmas Eve, such as leaving cookies out for Santa," says Glen. Incorporating grown-up cocktails and elegant red-and-silver decor, Gatsby's Christmas Eve soiree is fun enough for kids and sophisticated enough for adults.

Meet the Hosts

WHO: Glen Collins and Kimi Dallman of Gatsby
WHERE: Dallas, TX
THE LOOK: naughty and nice

GET KIMI & GLEN'S LOOK

1 | *Keep the party fare simple.*

To save time, serve a variety of store-bought desserts for a beautiful spread that's both easy and decadent. Gatsby set out rich chocolate-covered caramels (or "lumps of coal") on a modern acrylic block along with an array of other chocolate indulgences from Tart Bakery in Dallas.

2 | *Upgrade your paper.*

Even the paper cocktail napkins can advance your party's theme. Gatsby printed their napkins with "naughty and nice" confessions to Santa in the same font as the party's invitations.

3 | *Add no-fuss flourishes.*

Visit your own yard to create inspired and inexpensive flower arrangements. Gatsby mixed red roses, boxwood, and homegrown greenery in metallic vessels for a woodsy-meets-glitzy motif.

4 | *Go for the unexpected.*

Drawing their inspiration from humble chalkboard menus, Gatsby applied a lettered decal to an antique mirror for an elegant bar menu. The letters were easily removed after the party to restore the mirror to its original condition.

5 | *Take a stand.*

Bright red candies, cream-filled macarons, and tarts topped with berries subtly reflect the party's red-and-silver color scheme. They're served on a combination of interesting containers and stands.

6 | *Go for self-serve.*

Gatsby offers kir royales from a classic martini pitcher and also has a nonalcoholic pomegranate punch for underage revelers.

I took the recycling to the grocery store parking lot every single week.

I hid the oreos from my husband.

2

3

5

I've been good, for

GOODNESS SAKE

Thank you very much.

6

CHRISTMAS DAY BRUNCH

When Mary Alice Sublett was planning her own wedding years ago, she enjoyed the process so much that she went into business planning other people's big days. After a few years on her own, she joined forces with Amber Housley, who brought a passion for event design and printed materials to the company. Together, Mary Alice and Amber work with discerning Nashville clients to create personalized weddings and events that are anything but cookie-cutter. The holiday brunch seen here has a lively flair with its crisp red-and-blue color scheme and a subtle peppermint theme. "We incorporated vintage ideas with a modern twist," says Mary Alice. Thoughtful details such as a custom welcome sign and locally produced party favors make their Christmas brunch a merry and memorable one.

Meet the Hosts

WHO: Amber Housley (left) and Mary Alice Sublett

WHERE: Nashville, TN

THE LOOK: modern meets vintage

GET MARY ALICE & AMBER'S LOOK

1 | *Package premade desserts.*
Served in glass jars with latch lids and embellished with snowflake trimmings, these ice-cream desserts can be scooped ahead of time and stored in the freezer.

2 | *Set a colorful table.*
Antique-style white wooden chargers and beaded-edge dinner plates play up the party's vintage look. They're topped with vibrant bird motif salad plates and blue paper boxes, which serve as both place cards and party favors.

3 | *Wrap up local treats.*
Mary Alice and Amber boxed up tasty chocolate-dipped peppermint sticks from Nashville chocolatier The Cocoa Tree as sweet parting gifts. "A good budget for favors is about $5 to $7 per guest," says Mary Alice.

4 | *Elevate store-bought candies.*
Even simple candies seem special with thoughtful presentation. Friend and Nashville-based scrapbook maven Jenni Bowlin made homespun, typed identifiers for the "sweet treats" bar.

5 | *Stagger flowers on the table.*
As a casual alternative to a formal centerpiece, Mary Alice and Amber arranged multiple bouquets of red tulips, roses, and ranunculus in vintage milk-glass vessels for a monochromatic look with lots of texture.

6 | *Serve simple cocktails.*
In keeping with the peppermint theme, they made minty cocktails using peppermint schnapps and lemon-lime soft drink. For a fun touch, they garnished with peppermint candy stir sticks.

CHRISTMAS DINNER

Many years ago, Lynn Easton Andrews planned a Charlottesville, Virginia, bride's nuptials as a favor for a friend. The very next day, her phone began ringing with requests from wedding guests impressed by her keen eye and impeccable organization. Today Easton Events executes everything from small country weddings to swanky corporate functions. The Christmas dinner seen here has a dressy but approachable atmosphere featuring a neutral palette of golds, silvers, and creams and emphasizing texture. "I wanted the soiree to feel organic yet luxurious—sophisticated without putting on airs," says Lynn. The juxtaposition of earthy elements, such as cedar logs and bare tigerwood branches nestled in the chandelier, with more lavish touches, such as mother-of-pearl napkin rings and gold-edged china, makes for a fancy gathering with a cozy undertone. In the corner, a graceful Christmas tree continues the effect.

Meet the Host

WHO: Lynn Easton Andrews of Easton Events

WHERE: Charlottesville, VA

THE LOOK: earthy elegance

GET LYNN'S LOOK

1 | *Showcase heirloom decorations.*

The informal hutch is decked with tonal, vintage pieces such as the glass-bead wreath, reindeer figurine, and mercury-glass candlesticks that call to mind past generations and gatherings.

2 | *Reimagine household objects.*

Repurposed drawer knobs make eye-catching place card holders. (To secure the cards better, replace stock washers with wider ones.) Balancing the heft of the knobs, the cards themselves are inscribed in a light, casual hand.

3 | *Serve a signature beverage.*

To finish on a comfy note, Lynn offers a spicy after-dinner eggnog garnished with whipped cream, cinnamon, and nutmeg and served with cookies on a silver tray.

4 | *Add a touch of couture.*

The lustrous mother-of-pearl napkin rings (fashioned from taffeta ribbon looped through vintage belt buckles) offer a sleek counterpoint to the room's cedar logs, birchwood votives, and distressed mirrors. Varying the size and shape of the napkin rings keeps the effect from feeling too stuffy.

5 | *Special touches at each place.*

To make each place setting feel special, Lynn adds a few simple touches. She crafted chic place mats with inexpensive wallpaper. Each plate has its own flower arrangement crafted from stemware, roses, and greenery.

6 | *Mix mirrors and candlelight.*

An antique mirror maximizes the pretty light cast from votives nestled in birch candleholders and puts a fresh spin on the common centerpiece combo. To replicate the mirror's patina, ask your local glass shop to distress a new one by applying boric acid to the surface.

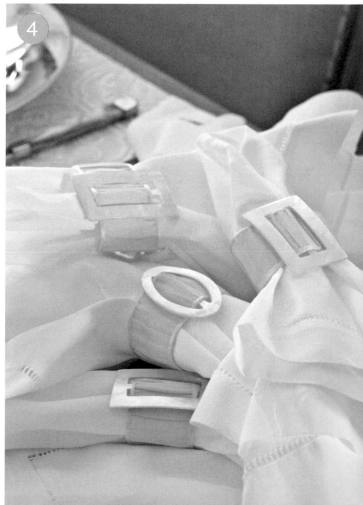

MERRY
STARTERS

Good friends and good food are a winning combination—especially during the holidays. This selection of appetizers and beverages makes any gathering more fun.

CRANBERRY-INFUSED MOONSHINE

MAKES: about 3¼ cups ▪ **HANDS-ON TIME:** 10 min. ▪ **TOTAL TIME:** 15 min., plus 3 days for infusing

1   cup fresh cranberries
¼   cup sugar
1   (350-milliliter) bottle moonshine
2   (2- x 1-inch) orange rind strips

Cook cranberries, sugar, and 3 Tbsp. water in a saucepan over medium heat 5 minutes or until sugar dissolves, liquid begins to turn a light pink color, and cranberries just begin to pop. Let cool slightly (about 10 minutes). Pour mixture into a large glass jar; stir in moonshine and 2 (2- x 1-inch) orange rind strips. Let stand at room temperature 3 days. Pour through a fine wire-mesh strainer into a bowl; discard solids. Return moonshine mixture to jar. Store in refrigerator up to 2 months.

FROZEN CRANBERRY-MOONSHINE LEMONADE

MAKES: 5 cups ▪ **HANDS-ON TIME:** 10 min. ▪ **TOTAL TIME:** 10 min.

1   (12-oz.) can frozen lemonade
        concentrate
¾   cup sweet-and-spicy moonshine
        or Cranberry-Infused Moonshine
⅓   cup whole-berry cranberry sauce
2   Tbsp. orange liqueur
2   Tbsp. fresh lime juice

Combine lemonade concentrate, moonshine or Cranberry-Infused Moonshine, whole-berry cranberry sauce, orange liqueur, and fresh lime juice in a blender. Fill with ice to 5-cup level; process until smooth.

CRANBERRY-MOONSHINE COCKTAIL

MAKES: 1 serving ▪ **HANDS-ON TIME:** 5 min. ▪ **TOTAL TIME:** 5 min.

3   Tbsp. Cranberry-Infused
        Moonshine
1   Tbsp. orange liqueur
1   (25.4-oz.) bottle blood orange
        Italian soda

Combine 2 cups ice cubes, Cranberry-Infused Moonshine, and liqueur in a cocktail shaker. Cover with lid, and shake until chilled. Remove lid, and strain into a chilled glass; top with chilled blood orange Italian soda. Serve immediately.

ULTIMATE ALEXANDER

One recipe fills the blender and will serve five to six people. Prepare two recipes to serve a party of 12.

MAKES: 5 cups ▪ **HANDS-ON TIME:** 5 min. ▪ **TOTAL TIME:** 5 min.

¼ cup cold brewed coffee
2 (14-oz.) containers coffee
   ice cream
½ cup brandy
½ cup chocolate syrup
Garnishes: wafer cookies, whipped
   topping, chocolate shavings

Process cold brewed coffee, ice cream, brandy, and chocolate syrup in a blender until smooth, stopping to scrape down sides. Pour mixture into glasses, and garnish, if desired. Serve immediately.

Note: *We tested with Häagen-Dazs Coffee ice cream and Pepperidge Farm Chocolate Fudge Pirouette Rolled Wafers.*

CRAN-BOURBON-AND-ORANGE REFRESHER

MAKES: 1 serving ▪ **HANDS-ON TIME:** 5 min. ▪ **TOTAL TIME:** 5 min.

3 Tbsp. bourbon
1 Tbsp. Cranberry Reduction
1 Tbsp. fresh orange juice
Club soda
Garnish: fresh rosemary sprig

Stir together bourbon, Cranberry Reduction, and fresh orange juice in a 10-oz. glass filled with ice cubes. Top with club soda. Garnish, if desired.

Cranberry Reduction

MAKES: 1¼ cups ▪ **HANDS-ON TIME:** 10 min. ▪ **TOTAL TIME:** 2 hours, 5 min.

2 cups cranberry juice
½ cup canned jellied cranberry
   sauce
¼ cup sugar
4 dashes of Angostura bitters
1 fresh rosemary sprig

Boil first 4 ingredients in a medium saucepan over medium heat, stirring often, 4 to 5 minutes or until smooth. Reduce heat to low, and simmer, stirring occasionally, 20 minutes or until liquid is reduced by half and slightly thickened. Add rosemary; cover and let stand 5 minutes. Discard rosemary. Cool mixture 30 minutes. Cover and chill 1 hour. Store in an airtight container in refrigerator for up to 1 week.

ULTIMATE ALEXANDER

CITRUS-MARINATED
FETA AND OLIVES

CITRUS-MARINATED FETA AND OLIVES

This gorgeous make-ahead dish is a crowd-pleaser at any gathering, and it's so easy to prepare.

MAKES: 6 to 8 servings ▪ **HANDS-ON TIME:** 10 min. ▪ **TOTAL TIME:** 10 min., plus 1 day for chilling

¼ cup chopped fresh basil
¼ cup olive oil
1 Tbsp. orange zest
1 tsp. coarsely ground pepper
1 garlic clove, minced
1 cup pitted kalamata olives
1 cup pimiento-stuffed
   Spanish olives
1 (8-oz.) feta cheese block, cubed

Whisk together first 5 ingredients in a medium-size glass bowl; gently stir in olives and cheese. Cover and chill 24 hours.

BARBECUE ROASTED NUTS

Two kinds of sugar sweeten this happy hour munchie. Buy shelled nuts to save time.

MAKES: 6 cups ▪ **HANDS-ON TIME:** 30 min. ▪ **TOTAL TIME:** 2 hours, 5 min.

2 egg whites
2 lb. assorted whole, raw nuts,
   shelled
1 Tbsp. kosher salt
1 Tbsp. light brown sugar
2 tsp. smoked paprika
1½ tsp. granulated sugar
½ tsp. garlic powder
½ tsp. dry mustard
¼ tsp. ground cumin
¼ tsp. ground ginger

Preheat oven to 350°. Whisk egg whites in a large bowl until foamy; toss nuts with whites. Stir together salt and next 7 ingredients; sprinkle over nuts, and toss to coat. Arrange nuts in a single layer in a 17- x 11-inch jelly-roll pan; bake at 350° for 25 to 30 minutes or until toasted and fragrant, stirring occasionally. Cool on a wire rack (about 1 hour). Store in airtight containers for up to 1 week.

HOT SPINACH-ARTICHOKE DIP

MAKES: 8 servings ▪ **HANDS-ON TIME:** 15 min. ▪ **TOTAL TIME:** 45 min.

1   cup freshly grated Parmesan
      cheese
1   cup reduced-fat sour cream
½   cup mayonnaise
4   green onions, sliced
3   Tbsp. fresh lemon juice
1   garlic clove, pressed
1¼   cups (5 oz.) shredded pepper
      Jack cheese
1   (10-oz.) package frozen chopped
      spinach, thawed and drained
1   (14-oz.) can artichoke hearts,
      drained and chopped
Freshly ground pepper to taste
Crackers
Assorted fresh vegetables

1. Preheat oven to 350°. Stir together first 6 ingredients and 1 cup pepper Jack cheese. Fold in spinach and artichokes. Spoon into a lightly greased 1-qt. baking dish. Sprinkle with remaining ¼ cup pepper Jack cheese.

2. Bake at 350° for 30 minutes or until center is hot and edges are bubbly. Add freshly ground pepper to taste. Serve with crackers and assorted fresh vegetables.

ROQUEFORT CHEESECAKE
with Pear Preserves and Pecans

MAKES: 12 appetizer servings ▪ **HANDS-ON TIME:** 15 min. ▪ **TOTAL TIME:** 9 hours, 55 min.

½   cup pecan or walnut halves
2   (8-oz.) packages cream cheese,
      softened
1   (8-oz.) package Roquefort
      cheese, chopped
½   cup sour cream
2   Tbsp. chopped fresh chives
1   Tbsp. chopped fresh parsley
2   large eggs
2   Tbsp. all-purpose flour
½   (11.5-oz.) jar pear preserves
Grapes

1. Preheat oven to 350°. Bake pecans in a single layer in a shallow pan 8 to 10 minutes or until lightly toasted, stirring halfway through. Reduce oven temperature to 325°.

2. Beat cream cheese and next 4 ingredients at medium speed with an electric mixer until blended. Add eggs, 1 at a time, beating just until yellow disappears; fold in flour. Spoon mixture into a lightly greased 7-inch springform pan.

3. Bake at 325° for 1 hour or until set. Run a knife around outer edge of cheesecake to loosen from sides of pan. Let cool in pan on a wire rack 30 minutes. Cover and chill 8 hours. Remove sides of pan. Transfer cheesecake to a platter, and spoon preserves over top; sprinkle with pecans. Serve with grapes.

ROQUEFORT CHEESECAKE

HOT SPINACH-
ARTICHOKE DIP

CHEESE RING

CHEESE RING
with Strawberry Preserves

MAKES: 8 to 10 servings ▪ **HANDS-ON TIME:** 20 min. ▪ **TOTAL TIME:** 2 hours, 45 min.

1 cup finely chopped pecans
¾ cup mayonnaise
½ tsp. hot sauce
1 garlic clove, minced
2 (8-oz.) blocks sharp Cheddar cheese, finely grated*
½ cup strawberry preserves
Assorted crackers
Garnishes: chopped toasted pecans, fresh strawberries, strawberry flowers

1. Preheat oven to 350°. Bake pecans in a single layer in a shallow pan 8 to 10 minutes or until toasted and fragrant, stirring halfway through. Cool 15 minutes.
2. Stir together mayonnaise and next 2 ingredients. Stir in pecans and cheese.
3. Spoon mixture into a plastic wrap-lined 4-cup ring mold with a 2 ½-inch center. Cover and chill 2 hours.
4. Unmold cheese ring onto a serving platter. Discard plastic wrap. Fill center of ring with preserves. Serve with crackers. Garnish, if desired.

Sharp white Cheddar cheese may be substituted.

SUN-DRIED TOMATO MARINATED BOCCONCINI IN GARLIC OIL

MAKES: 7 half pints ▪ **HANDS-ON TIME:** 17 min. ▪ **TOTAL TIME:** 24 hours, 17 min.

1 (7-oz.) jar sun-dried tomatoes in oil
1 cup olive oil
¾ cup white wine vinegar
1 Tbsp. fresh thyme leaves
1 tsp. freshly ground pepper
¾ tsp. salt
5 garlic cloves, coarsely chopped
2 lb. bocconcini mozzarella, drained
7 (½-pt.) jars, sterilized

Drain tomatoes, reserving oil. Chop tomatoes. Process tomato oil, olive oil, and next 5 ingredients in a blender until smooth. Pour into a bowl; stir in chopped tomatoes. Add cheese, stirring to coat. Fill jars with cheese, and marinate in refrigerator at least 24 hours before serving. Store in refrigerator up to 1 week.

TORTELLINI CAPRESE BITES

Tortellini Caprese Bites, drizzled with a basil vinaigrette, are so simple to prepare. The no-mess presentation makes these appetizer skewers ideal for parties.

MAKES: 12 servings ▪ **HANDS-ON TIME:** 30 min. ▪ **TOTAL TIME:** 2 hours, 47 min.

1 (9-oz.) package refrigerated cheese-filled tortellini
3 cups halved grape tomatoes
3 (8-oz.) containers fresh small mozzarella cheese balls
60 (6-inch) wooden skewers
Basil Vinaigrette

1. Prepare tortellini according to package directions. Rinse under cold running water.
2. Thread 1 tomato half, 1 cheese ball, another tomato half, and 1 tortellini onto each skewer. Place skewers in a 13- x 9-inch baking dish. Pour Basil Vinaigrette over skewers, turning to coat. Cover and chill 2 hours. Transfer skewers to a serving platter, and add salt and pepper to taste. Discard any remaining vinaigrette.

Note: *We tested with Whole Foods Ciliegine Fresh Mozzarella Cheese.*

Basil Vinaigrette

MAKES: 1½ cups ▪ **HANDS-ON TIME:** 10 min. ▪ **TOTAL TIME:** 10 min.

½ cup white balsamic vinegar
1 tsp. kosher salt
⅔ cup extra virgin olive oil
6 Tbsp. chopped fresh basil

Whisk together vinegar and salt until blended. Gradually add oil in a slow, steady stream, whisking constantly until smooth. Stir in basil and freshly ground pepper to taste.

HONEY-ROSEMARY CHERRIES AND BLUE CHEESE CROSTINI

MAKES: 8 appetizer servings ▪ **HANDS-ON TIME:** 20 min. ▪ **TOTAL TIME:** 30 min.

1   shallot, thinly sliced
2   tsp. olive oil
1   (12-oz.) package frozen dark,
       sweet pitted cherries, thawed
2   Tbsp. balsamic vinegar
2   Tbsp. honey
¼   tsp. chopped fresh rosemary
⅛   tsp. salt
⅛   tsp. pepper
2   cups loosely packed arugula
16   (¼-inch-thick) ciabatta bread
       slices, toasted
1   (8-oz.) wedge blue cheese,
       thinly sliced*
Garnish: freshly ground black
       pepper

1. Sauté shallot in hot oil in a medium skillet over medium-high heat 2 to 3 minutes or until tender. Add cherries (and any liquid in package) and next 5 ingredients. Cook, stirring occasionally, 8 to 10 minutes or until thickened. Let stand 10 minutes.

2. Divide arugula evenly among toasted bread slices. Top each with cherry mixture and 1 blue cheese slice.

*Manchego or goat cheese may be substituted.

Begin your party casually by offering this appetizer "help yourself" style. Or make single-serving plates, and present them as a first course at the table.

PEPPER JACK-GRITS POPPERS

MAKES: about 10 appetizer servings ▪ **HANDS-ON TIME:** 35 min. ▪ **TOTAL TIME:** 8 hours, 40 min.

1   cup hot cooked grits
1   cup (4 oz.) freshly shredded
      pepper Jack cheese
½   cup shredded Parmesan cheese
2   Tbsp. chopped fresh cilantro
1   garlic clove, pressed
18 to 20 sweet mini bell peppers

1. Stir together first 5 ingredients until cheese melts; add salt and pepper to taste. Cover and chill 8 hours.
2. Preheat broiler with oven rack 6 inches from heat. Cut peppers in half lengthwise, leaving stems intact; remove seeds. Spoon grits mixture into pepper halves. Place on a broiler pan. Broil 4 minutes or until golden brown.

CHEESE-AND-BACON OKRA POPPERS

We loved the bacon-wrapped pods, but you can save prep time by crumbling the bacon into the cheese mixture, stuffing the pods, and baking.

MAKES: 16 servings ▪ **HANDS-ON TIME:** 20 min. ▪ **TOTAL TIME:** 44 min.

16   bacon slices
1   lb. fresh okra (32 pods)
1   (8-oz.) container chive-and-
      onion cream cheese, softened
½   cup shredded extra-sharp
      Cheddar cheese
¼   cup chopped green onions
¼   tsp. kosher salt
¼   tsp. freshly ground pepper
Vegetable cooking spray

1. Preheat oven to 425° with oven rack 6 inches from heat. Cook bacon, in 2 batches, in a large skillet over medium-high heat 1 to 2 minutes on each side or just until bacon begins to curl; remove bacon, and drain on paper towels. Cut each slice in half crosswise. Discard drippings.
2. Cut each okra pod lengthwise down 1 side, leaving stem and other side of pod intact; remove seeds and membranes.
3. Stir together cream cheese and next 4 ingredients in a small bowl. Carefully pipe cheese mixture into cavity of each okra pod. Wrap each stuffed okra pod with 1 bacon piece, and secure with a wooden pick.
4. Place half of okra, cheese side up, on a foil-lined baking sheet coated with cooking spray. Bake at 425° for 8 minutes or until okra is tender and bacon is crisp. Transfer to a serving platter; keep warm. Repeat procedure with remaining half of okra. Serve warm.

CHEESE-AND-BACON
OKRA POPPERS

PEPPER JELLY-PECAN RUGELACH

MAKES: about 5 dozen ▪ **HANDS-ON TIME:** 30 min. ▪ **TOTAL TIME:** 3 hours, 15 min.

2¼ cups all-purpose flour
1 cup cold butter, cut into pieces
1 (8-oz.) package cream cheese,
    cut into pieces
½ tsp. salt
1 (10-oz.) jar red pepper jelly
1 cup finely chopped
    toasted pecans
Parchment paper

1. Pulse first 4 ingredients in a food processor 3 or 4 times or until dough forms a ball and leaves sides of bowl. Divide dough into 8 portions, shaping each into a ball. Wrap each separately in plastic wrap; chill 1 to 24 hours.
2. Preheat oven to 375°. Cook pepper jelly in a small saucepan over medium heat, stirring often, 2 to 3 minutes or just until melted.
3. Roll 1 dough ball into an 8-inch circle on a lightly floured surface. Brush dough with 1 to 2 Tbsp. melted jelly; sprinkle with 2 Tbsp. pecans. Cut circle into 8 wedges, and roll up wedges, starting at wide end, to form a crescent shape. Place, point sides down, on a lightly greased parchment paper-lined baking sheet. Repeat procedure with remaining dough balls, pepper jelly, and pecans.
4. Bake at 375° for 15 to 20 minutes or until golden brown. Transfer to wire racks. Cool completely (30 minutes).

PLAN AHEAD

Make these crunchy treats ahead of time and serve at room temperature. They're a perfect holiday pickup food.

CHICKEN SALAD PITAS

MAKES: 4 dozen ▪ **HANDS-ON TIME:** 30 min. ▪ **TOTAL TIME:** 4 hours, 30 min.

½ cup mayonnaise
⅓ cup red pepper jelly
¼ cup minced green onions
2 Tbsp. chopped fresh cilantro
1 tsp. lime zest
¼ tsp. ground red pepper
2 cups finely chopped
   cooked chicken
½ cup finely chopped celery
½ cup finely chopped
   toasted pecans
24 mini pita pockets, halved
1 bunch fresh watercress

Whisk together first 6 ingredients in a large bowl; stir in chicken and next 2 ingredients until blended. Add salt and pepper to taste. Cover and chill 4 hours. Fill pitas with watercress and chicken salad. Serve immediately.

TUNA-APPLE MINI MELTS

MAKES: 45 tartlets ▪ **HANDS-ON TIME:** 30 min. ▪ **TOTAL TIME:** 1 hour, 30 min.

1 cup mayonnaise
½ cup diced Pink Lady apple*
⅓ cup finely chopped celery
2 Tbsp. minced red onion
1 hard-cooked egg, peeled
   and chopped
1 tsp. fresh lemon juice
¼ tsp. kosher salt
¼ tsp. freshly ground pepper
2 (12-oz.) cans solid white tuna
   in spring water, drained
   and flaked
3 (1.9-oz.) packages frozen mini-
   phyllo pastry shells, thawed
12 deli Havarti cheese slices,
   cut into 4 pieces each
Garnish: thin Pink Lady apple slices

1. Stir together first 8 ingredients in a medium bowl. Stir in tuna. Cover and chill 1 hour.
2. Divide mixture among phyllo shells (about 1 Tbsp. each), and place on a 15- x 10-inch jelly-roll pan. Top with cheese pieces.
3. Preheat broiler with oven rack 5½ inches from heat. Broil tartlets 1 to 2 minutes or until cheese melts. Serve immediately.

*Gala apple may be substituted.

CHICKEN SALAD PITAS

TINY TOMATO TARTS

TINY TOMATO TARTS

MAKES: 24 tartlets ▪ HANDS-ON TIME: 30 min. ▪ TOTAL TIME: 50 min.

½ (14.1-oz.) package
    refrigerated piecrusts
1 (14.5-oz.) can petite
    diced tomatoes
1 Tbsp. chopped fresh basil
⅔ cup mayonnaise
½ cup grated Parmesan cheese
¼ cup (1 oz.) freshly shredded
    Cheddar cheese
¼ cup (1 oz.) freshly shredded
    mozzarella cheese
Garnish: fresh basil leaves

1. Preheat oven to 425°. Unroll piecrust on a lightly floured surface; roll into a 12-inch circle. Cut into 24 rounds using a 2-inch scalloped-edge round cutter. Press rounds into bottoms of ungreased miniature muffin cups. (Dough will come slightly up sides, forming a cup.) Prick bottom of dough once with a fork.
2. Bake at 425° for 4 to 5 minutes or until set. Cool in pans on a wire rack 15 minutes. Reduce oven temperature to 350°.
3. Meanwhile, drain tomatoes well, pressing between paper towels. Combine tomatoes and chopped basil in a small bowl; add salt and pepper to taste. Stir together mayonnaise and next 3 ingredients in a medium bowl. Divide tomato mixture among pastry shells, and top with mayonnaise mixture.
4. Bake at 350° for 18 to 20 minutes. Serve immediately.

Make Ahead: *To make ahead, bake and cool pastry shells as directed in Steps 1 and 2. Remove from muffin pans, and store in an airtight container for up to 3 days. Return pastry shells to muffin pans; fill and bake as directed.*

MUSHROOM PUFFS

MAKES: about 3 dozen ▪ HANDS-ON TIME: 30 min. ▪ TOTAL TIME: 1 hour, 50 min.

1 (8-oz.) package cream cheese,
    softened
1 (8-oz.) can mushroom
    pieces and stems, drained
    and chopped
¼ cup finely chopped onion
¼ cup grated Parmesan cheese
1 Tbsp. finely chopped green onion
¼ tsp. hot sauce
1 large egg
1 (17.3-oz.) package frozen
    puff pastry sheets, thawed
Parchment paper
2 tsp. freshly ground pepper

1. Beat cream cheese at medium speed with a heavy-duty electric stand mixer until smooth. Stir in mushrooms and next 4 ingredients. Cover and chill 1 to 24 hours.
2. Preheat oven to 400°. Whisk together egg and 1 Tbsp. water in a small bowl. Roll 1 puff pastry sheet into a 16- x 10-inch rectangle on a lightly floured surface. Cut pastry in half lengthwise. Spread ½ cup cream cheese mixture down center of each rectangle; brush edges with egg mixture. Fold each pastry half lengthwise over filling, and pinch edges to seal. Cut pastries into 10 pieces each, and place on a parchment paper-lined baking sheet. Repeat procedure with remaining puff pastry sheet, egg mixture, and cream cheese mixture.
3. Brush remaining egg mixture over tops of pastry pieces; sprinkle with pepper.
4. Bake at 400° for 20 to 25 minutes or until browned. Serve immediately.

Make Ahead: *To make ahead, prepare recipe as directed through Step 3. Freeze pieces on baking sheet until firm (about 1 hour), and transfer to zip-top plastic freezer bags. Freeze for up to 1 month. To bake, place frozen puffs on parchment paper-lined baking sheets, and proceed as directed in Step 4.*

BACON-WRAPPED SHRIMP

MAKES: 2 dozen ▪ **HANDS-ON TIME:** 20 min. ▪ **TOTAL TIME:** 1 hour

24   unpeeled, large raw shrimp
¼   cup canola oil
¼   cup balsamic vinegar
3   Tbsp. chopped fresh basil
2   shallots, minced
1   garlic clove, minced
1   Tbsp. light brown sugar
¼   tsp. ground red pepper
⅛   tsp. salt
12   bacon slices, cut in half crosswise
24   wooden picks

1. Preheat oven to 450°. Peel and devein shrimp, leaving tails on. Combine canola oil and next 7 ingredients in a zip-top plastic freezer bag. Add shrimp; seal and chill 30 minutes, turning once.

2. Meanwhile, arrange bacon in a single layer in a 15- x- 10-inch jelly-roll pan. Bake at 450° for 6 to 8 minutes or just until bacon begins to brown. (Bacon will be partially cooked, not crisp.) Remove from pan, and drain on paper towels. Reduce oven temperature to 400°.

3. Place a lightly greased wire rack in an aluminum foil-lined 15- x 10-inch jelly-roll pan. Remove shrimp from marinade; discard marinade. Wrap 1 bacon piece around each shrimp, and secure with a wooden pick threaded through both ends of shrimp. Arrange shrimp in a single layer on wire rack.

4. Bake at 400° for 8 to 10 minutes or until bacon is crisp and shrimp turn pink. Serve immediately.

BACON-WRAPPED BOURBON FIGS

MAKES: 2 dozen ▪ **HANDS-ON TIME:** 20 min. ▪ **TOTAL TIME:** 55 min.

12   dried Calimyrna figs
¼   cup bourbon
1   (2- to 4-oz.) wedge Gorgonzola
     cheese, cut into 24 pieces
24   pecan halves, toasted
12   fully cooked bacon slices,
     cut in half crosswise
24   wooden picks

1. Combine first 2 ingredients and 1½ cups water in a medium saucepan. Cook, covered, over low heat 15 to 20 minutes or until figs are plump and softened. Remove from heat; cool slightly (about 15 minutes). Drain figs; gently pat dry with paper towels.

2. Preheat oven to 350°. Cut figs in half lengthwise. Place 1 cheese piece and 1 pecan half on cut side of each fig half. Wrap 1 bacon piece around each fig, and secure with a wooden pick. Place on a wire rack in a 15- x 10-inch jelly-roll pan.

3. Bake at 350° for 6 to 8 minutes or until bacon is crisp and browned.

Note: *We tested with Oscar Mayer Fully Cooked Bacon.*

BACON-WRAPPED SHRIMP

BACON-WRAPPED
BOURBON FIGS

CHICKEN-AND-BACON SATAY

Satay is an Indonesian version of kabobs. Thinly sliced marinated meat is grilled on a skewer and served with peanut sauce.

MAKES: 16 to 20 ▪ **HANDS-ON TIME:** 40 min. ▪ **TOTAL TIME:** 1 hour, 35 min.

4 skinned and boned chicken
    thighs (about 1 lb.)
½ cup lite soy sauce
⅓ cup sake
2 Tbsp. light brown sugar
1 Tbsp. grated fresh ginger
½ tsp. dried crushed red pepper
16 to 20 (4-inch) wooden skewers
8 to 10 fully cooked bacon slices,
    cut in half crosswise
Peanut Sauce
Garnish: thinly sliced green onions

1. Place chicken between 2 sheets of plastic wrap, and flatten to ¼-inch thickness using a rolling pin or flat side of a meat mallet. Cut chicken into 16 to 20 (1-inch) strips.

2. Combine soy sauce and next 4 ingredients in a large zip-top plastic freezer bag; add chicken, turning to coat. Seal and chill 45 minutes, turning once.

3. Meanwhile, soak skewers in water 30 minutes; drain.

4. Preheat grill to 350° to 400° (medium-high) heat. Remove chicken from marinade; discard marinade. Thread 1 bacon piece and 1 chicken strip onto each skewer.

5. Grill skewers, covered with grill lid, 4 to 5 minutes on each side or until chicken is desired degree of doneness. Serve skewers with Peanut Sauce.

Peanut Sauce

MAKES: 1⅓ cups ▪ **HANDS-ON TIME:** 10 min. ▪ **TOTAL TIME:** 10 min.

½ cup creamy peanut butter
⅓ cup lite soy sauce
¼ cup loosely packed fresh cilantro
    leaves
3 Tbsp. fresh lime juice
3 Tbsp. honey
3 Tbsp. dark sesame oil

Process peanut butter, soy sauce, cilantro, lime juice, honey, and dark sesame oil in a blender or food processor until smooth. Add 1 to 2 Tbsp. water, 1 tsp. at a time, processing until desired consistency is reached.

BACON-WRAPPED POTATOES
with *Queso Blanco Dip*

MAKES: 8 servings ▪ **HANDS-ON TIME:** 30 min. ▪ **TOTAL TIME:** 1 hour, 30 min.

2   medium-size red potatoes,
    cut into 8 wedges each
½   tsp. salt
16 center-cut bacon slices
½   tsp. pepper
½   cup diced red onion
1   Tbsp. canola oil
1   garlic clove, minced
12 oz. queso blanco pasteurized
    prepared cheese product,
    cubed
1   (8-oz.) block pepper Jack
    cheese, shredded
½   cup half-and-half
1   (4-oz.) can chopped green chiles
1   plum tomato, seeded and diced
¼   cup chopped fresh cilantro

1. Preheat oven to 425°. Sprinkle potato wedges with salt. Wrap each with 1 bacon slice. Arrange potato wedges in a single layer on a lightly greased wire rack in an aluminum foil-lined 15- x 10-inch jelly-roll pan. Sprinkle with pepper.

2. Bake at 425° for 40 to 45 minutes or until bacon is crisp and browned.

3. Meanwhile, sauté onion in hot oil in a small nonstick skillet over medium-high heat 5 minutes or until tender. Add garlic, and sauté 1 minute. Remove from heat.

4. Combine queso blanco, next 3 ingredients, and onion mixture in a large microwave-safe glass bowl. Microwave at HIGH 2½ minutes; stir and microwave 2½ more minutes or until cheese melts and mixture is smooth, stirring at 1-minute intervals.

5. Stir diced tomato and cilantro into queso blanco mixture. Serve dip with potato wedges.

Note: We tested with Velveeta Queso Blanco for prepared cheese product.

You can keep the Queso Blanco Dip warm in a fondue pot or 1-qt. slow cooker. This hearty appetizer will score points at a tailgate party!

MINI CRAB CAKES

MAKES: 8 servings ▪ **HANDS-ON TIME:** 30 min. ▪ **TOTAL TIME:** 1 hour, 30 min.

1½ lb. fresh crabmeat, drained
¼ cup mayonnaise
1 large egg
1 Tbsp. Dijon mustard
1 tsp. lemon zest
¼ cup panko (Japanese
    breadcrumbs)
3 Tbsp. minced green onions
3 Tbsp. diced red bell pepper
4 Tbsp. butter
Pineapple-Cucumber Salsa

1. Pick crabmeat, removing any bits of shell.
2. Whisk together mayonnaise and next 3 ingredients in a large bowl. Gently stir in crabmeat, panko, and next 2 ingredients. Shape mixture into 16 (2-inch) cakes (about ¼ cup each). Cover and chill 1 to 4 hours.
3. Melt 2 Tbsp. butter in a large nonstick skillet over medium heat. Add 8 crab cakes; cook 2 to 3 minutes on each side or until browned. Repeat with remaining butter and crab cakes. Serve with Pineapple-Cucumber Salsa.

Pineapple-Cucumber Salsa

MAKES: 3¾ cups ▪ **HANDS-ON TIME:** 20 min. ▪ **TOTAL TIME:** 1 hour, 20 min.

2 cups diced fresh pineapple
1 English cucumber, peeled
    and diced (about 1½ cups)
2 green onions, thinly sliced
    (about ¼ cup)
1 jalapeño pepper, seeded
    and minced
¼ cup chopped fresh basil
1 Tbsp. fresh lime juice
⅛ tsp. salt

Combine all ingredients in a large bowl, stirring gently to mix. Cover and chill 1 to 24 hours.

FINGERLING POTATOES
with Avocado and Smoked Salmon

MAKES: 8 servings ▪ **HANDS-ON TIME:** 15 min. ▪ **TOTAL TIME:** 55 min.

1   lb. fingerling potatoes,
       halved lengthwise
1   Tbsp. olive oil
½   tsp. salt
¼   tsp. pepper
1   ripe avocado, halved
1   Tbsp. minced fresh dill weed
1   tsp. lemon zest
2   tsp. fresh lemon juice
⅛   tsp. salt
1   (4-oz.) package thinly sliced
       smoked salmon
Garnish: fresh dill sprigs

1. Preheat oven to 400°. Toss together first 4 ingredients. Place potatoes, cut sides down, in a lightly greased jelly-roll pan. Bake at 400° for 20 minutes or until tender and browned. Cool completely (about 20 minutes).
2. Meanwhile, scoop avocado pulp into a bowl; mash with a fork. Stir in dill weed and next 3 ingredients. Spoon mixture onto cut sides of potatoes, and top each with 1 salmon slice.

You'll love the unexpected flavor combination of creamy avocado and fresh dill atop roasted potatoes.

PORK TENDERLOIN
CROSTINI

PEPPER JELLY-GOAT CHEESE
CAKES (PAGE 58)

PORK TENDERLOIN CROSTINI

MAKES: 4 dozen ▪ **HANDS-ON TIME:** 30 min. ▪ **TOTAL TIME:** 2 hours, 50 min.

24 *frozen tea biscuits*
2 *(³/₄- to 1-lb.) pork tenderloins*
1 *tsp. salt*
2 *tsp. freshly ground pepper*
2 *Tbsp. olive oil*
5 *Tbsp. butter, melted*
Cranberry-Pepper Jelly
1 *bunch fresh watercress*

1. Preheat oven to 350°. Bake tea biscuits according to package directions. Cool on a wire rack 20 minutes.
2. Preheat grill to 350° to 400° (medium-high) heat. Remove silver skin from each tenderloin. Sprinkle salt and pepper over pork; rub with olive oil. Grill pork, covered with grill lid, 10 to 12 minutes on each side or until a meat thermometer inserted into thickest portion registers 145°. Remove from grill; cover with aluminum foil, and let stand 15 minutes.
3. Meanwhile, cut biscuits in half, and brush cut sides with melted butter. Arrange, cut sides up, on a baking sheet. Bake at 350° for 8 to 10 minutes or until edges are golden.
4. Cut pork into ¼-inch-thick slices (about 24 slices each). Place pork on biscuit halves; top with desired amount of Cranberry-Pepper Jelly and watercress sprigs. Serve immediately.

Cranberry-Pepper Jelly

MAKES: 3 cups ▪ **HANDS-ON TIME:** 25 min. ▪ **TOTAL TIME:** 1 hour, 10 min.

1 *(12-oz.) package fresh cranberries*
1 *(10-oz.) jar red pepper jelly*
1½ *cups peeled and diced Granny Smith apple*
¾ *cup sugar*
¼ *tsp. dried crushed red pepper*
½ *cup sweetened dried cranberries*

Bring fresh cranberries, jelly, apple, sugar, ½ cup water, and crushed red pepper to a boil in a large saucepan over medium-high heat, stirring often. Reduce heat to medium-low, and simmer, stirring often, 10 to 15 minutes or until cranberries begin to pop and mixture starts to thicken. Remove from heat, and stir in sweetened dried cranberries. Cool completely (about 45 minutes). Serve at room temperature, or cover and chill 8 hours before serving. Store in an airtight container in refrigerator for up to 2 weeks.

PEPPER JELLY-GOAT CHEESE CAKES

pictured on page 56

MAKES: 2 dozen ▪ **HANDS-ON TIME:** 20 min. ▪ **TOTAL TIME:** 2 hours, 50 min.

24 aluminum foil miniature
    baking cups
Vegetable cooking spray
¼ cup fine, dry Italian-seasoned
    breadcrumbs
¼ cup ground toasted pecans
2 Tbsp. grated Parmesan cheese
2 Tbsp. butter, melted
1 (8-oz.) package cream cheese,
    softened
1 (4-oz.) goat cheese log, softened
1 large egg
2 Tbsp. heavy cream
1 Tbsp. Asian hot chili sauce
    (such as Sriracha)
¼ cup green pepper jelly, melted
¼ cup red pepper jelly, melted

1. Preheat oven to 350°. Place baking cups in 2 (12-cup) miniature muffin pans; coat baking cups with cooking spray.

2. Stir together breadcrumbs and next 3 ingredients. Firmly press about 1 tsp. breadcrumb mixture in bottom of each baking cup.

3. Beat cream cheese and goat cheese at medium speed with an electric mixer until light and fluffy; add egg and next 2 ingredients, beating just until blended. Spoon into baking cups, filling three-fourths full.

4. Bake at 350° for 10 minutes or until set. Cool completely in pans on a wire rack (about 20 minutes). Spoon 1 tsp. melted green pepper jelly over each of 12 cheesecakes. Spoon 1 tsp. melted red pepper jelly over each of remaining 12 cheesecakes. Cover and chill 2 to 12 hours before serving.

Tip: *To melt pepper jellies, microwave them in a microwave-safe bowl at HIGH for 20 to 25 seconds.*

SHRIMP AND CITRUS COCKTAIL

Give this updated classic a fresh look by serving it in modern stemmed glassware.

MAKES: 4 to 6 servings ▪ **HANDS-ON TIME:** 15 min. ▪ **TOTAL TIME:** 3 hours, 15 min.

1 lb. peeled, large cooked
    shrimp with tails
⅓ cup olive oil
⅓ cup red wine vinegar
2 large shallots, minced
2 tsp. Dijon mustard
2 tsp. orange zest
½ tsp. salt
½ tsp. dried crushed red pepper
2 large navel oranges, peeled
    and sectioned
3 Tbsp. chopped fresh basil

1. Devein shrimp, if desired.

2. Whisk together olive oil and next 6 ingredients in a large bowl. Pour mixture into a large zip-top plastic freezer bag; add shrimp, turning to coat. Seal and chill 3 to 8 hours, turning occasionally. Remove shrimp from marinade; discard marinade. Combine shrimp, oranges and basil. Spoon mixture into chilled glasses or small serving bowls.

SHRIMP AND CITRUS
COCKTAIL

SALT-ROASTED BEEF TENDERLOIN SLIDERS

MAKES: 8 servings ▪ **HANDS-ON TIME:** 20 min. ▪ **TOTAL TIME:** 1 hour, 25 min.

1   (1½-lb.) beef tenderloin, trimmed
1   tsp. cracked pepper
1   Tbsp. olive oil
6   cups kosher salt
1   cup cold water
24 small rolls or buns, split and
       toasted
Chimichurri Pesto
4   plum tomatoes, thinly sliced

1. Preheat oven to 400°. Sprinkle beef with pepper. Cook in hot oil in a skillet over medium-high heat, turning occasionally, 5 minutes or until browned on all sides.
2. Stir together salt and 1 cup cold water. Spread half of salt mixture in a rectangle (slightly larger than beef) in a large roasting pan; top with beef. Pat remaining salt mixture over beef, covering completely.
3. Bake at 400° 45 to 50 minutes or until a meat thermometer inserted into center registers 145°. Remove crust. (Beef will keep cooking if crust remains on.) Transfer beef to a cutting board. Cover loosely with aluminum foil; let stand 10 minutes. Brush off excess salt; slice beef. Serve beef in rolls with pesto and sliced tomatoes.

Chimichurri Pesto

MAKES: about 1 cup ▪ **HANDS-ON TIME:** 10 min. ▪ **TOTAL TIME:** 10 min.

1   cup firmly packed fresh flat-leaf
       parsley leaves
1   cup firmly packed fresh cilantro
       leaves
½   cup chopped toasted walnuts
½   cup freshly grated Parmesan
       cheese
1   tsp. fresh lemon juice
1   small garlic clove, chopped
¼   tsp. salt
¼   tsp. dried crushed red pepper
¼   cup extra virgin olive oil

Process parsley leaves, cilantro leaves, walnuts, Parmesan cheese, fresh lemon juice, garlic, salt, and red pepper in a food processor until finely chopped. With processor running, pour olive oil through food chute in a slow, steady stream, processing until smooth.

SEASONAL SIDES & SALADS

Round out your meal with these colorful and tasty dishes. From classic mashed potatoes to green beans with a twist, there's something for every occasion.

CRISPY GOAT CHEESE-TOPPED ARUGULA SALAD

MAKES: 8 servings ▪ **HANDS-ON TIME:** 25 min. ▪ **TOTAL TIME:** 1 hour, 50 min., including vinaigrette

4   (4-oz.) goat cheese logs
½   cup all-purpose flour
½   tsp. freshly ground black pepper
2   egg whites
1   cup panko (Japanese breadcrumbs)
4   Tbsp. olive oil
2   (5-oz.) containers baby
    arugula
4   large navel oranges, peeled
    and sectioned
Pomegranate Vinaigrette
Garnish: pomegranate seeds

1. Cut each goat cheese log into 6 (½-inch-wide) slices. Combine flour and black pepper in a shallow dish. Whisk together egg whites and 2 Tbsp. water in another shallow dish. Place panko in a third shallow dish. Dredge goat cheese in flour mixture, dip in egg mixture, and dredge in panko. Arrange goat cheese in a single layer in an aluminum foil-lined jelly-roll pan; cover and chill 30 minutes to 4 hours.

2. Cook half of goat cheese rounds in 2 Tbsp. hot oil in a large nonstick skillet over medium heat 2 to 3 minutes on each side or until lightly browned; drain on paper towels. Repeat with remaining oil and goat cheese rounds.

3. Divide arugula and orange sections among 8 plates; drizzle with Pomegranate Vinaigrette. Top each salad with 3 goat cheese rounds.

Tip: *To get clean slices of cheese, dip the knife in hot water.*

Pomegranate Vinaigrette

MAKES: ⅔ cup ▪ **HANDS-ON TIME:** 20 min. ▪ **TOTAL TIME:** 55 min.

1½   cups pomegranate juice
⅓   cup olive oil
5   tsp. honey
1   Tbsp. white wine vinegar
1   tsp. Dijon mustard
¼   tsp. freshly ground black pepper

Bring 1½ cups pomegranate juice to a boil in a medium saucepan over medium-high heat; reduce heat to medium, and cook, stirring occasionally, 15 minutes or until reduced to ¼ cup. Transfer to a small bowl. Cool completely (about 30 minutes). Whisk in oil and next 4 ingredients. Add salt to taste.

ARUGULA-PEAR-BLUE CHEESE SALAD

MAKES: 8 servings ▪ **HANDS-ON TIME:** 15 min. ▪ **TOTAL TIME:** 15 min.

¼ cup pear preserves
½ cup Champagne vinegar
1 shallot, sliced
2 tsp. Dijon mustard
½ tsp. table salt
¼ tsp. freshly ground black pepper
½ cup olive oil
2 Tbsp. pear preserves
8 cups loosely packed arugula
2 Bartlett pears, cut into
   6 wedges each
4 oz. blue cheese, crumbled
¼ cup chopped toasted walnuts

1. Process ¼ cup preserves and next 5 ingredients in a food processor 30 seconds to 1 minute or until smooth. With food processor running, pour oil through food chute in a slow steady stream, processing until smooth. Transfer to a 2-cup measuring cup or small bowl, and stir in 2 Tbsp. pear preserves.
2. Place arugula in a large serving bowl. Top with pears, blue cheese, and walnuts. Drizzle with vinaigrette.

HERBS AND GREENS SALAD

MAKES: 6 to 8 servings ▪ **HANDS-ON TIME:** 10 min. ▪ **TOTAL TIME:** 30 min.

½ tsp. lemon zest
4 Tbsp. olive oil, divided
3 cups 1-inch olive bread cubes*
4 cups torn butter lettuce
   (about 1 head)
2 cups firmly packed fresh baby
   spinach
1 cup torn escarole
½ cup loosely packed fresh
   parsley leaves
¼ cup fresh 1-inch chive pieces
2 Tbsp. fresh lemon juice

1. Preheat oven to 425°. Stir together lemon zest and 1 Tbsp. olive oil in a large bowl. Add bread cubes, and toss to coat. Arrange in a single layer on a baking sheet. Bake at 425° for 5 minutes or until crisp. Cool completely (about 15 minutes).
2. Meanwhile, combine butter lettuce and next 4 ingredients in a large bowl. Drizzle with lemon juice and remaining 3 Tbsp. olive oil, and toss to coat. Add salt and pepper to taste. Serve immediately with toasted bread cubes.

*Ciabatta, focaccia, or country white bread may be substituted.

ARUGULA-PEAR-BLUE
CHEESE SALAD

FRESH PEAR-AND-GREEN BEAN SALAD

MAKES: 8 servings ▪ **HANDS-ON TIME:** 15 min. ▪ **TOTAL TIME:** 1 hour, 15 min.

8   oz. haricots verts (thin green beans), trimmed
1   (5-oz.) package gourmet mixed salad greens
2   red Bartlett pears, cut into thin strips
½   small red onion, sliced
2   cups Sweet and Spicy Pecans
4   oz. Gorgonzola cheese, crumbled
Sorghum Vinaigrette

Cook beans in boiling salted water to cover 3 to 4 minutes or until crisp-tender; drain. Plunge beans into ice water to stop cooking process; drain. Toss together salad greens, next 4 ingredients, and beans. Serve with Sorghum Vinaigrette.

Sweet and Spicy Pecans

MAKES: 2 cups ▪ **HANDS-ON TIME:** 10 min. ▪ **TOTAL TIME:** 55 min.

¼   cup sorghum syrup
2   Tbsp. Demerara sugar
½   tsp. kosher salt
¼   tsp. ground red pepper
2   cups pecan halves
Parchment paper

1. Preheat oven to 350°. Stir together first 4 ingredients. Add pecan halves; stir until coated. Line a jelly-roll pan with parchment paper, and lightly grease paper. Arrange pecans in a single layer in pan.
2. Bake at 350° for 15 minutes or until glaze bubbles slowly and thickens, stirring once after 8 minutes. Transfer pan to a wire rack. Separate pecans into individual pieces; cool completely in pan, about 35 minutes. If cooled pecans are not crisp, bake 5 more minutes.

Sorghum Vinaigrette

MAKES: 2 cups ▪ **HANDS-ON TIME:** 5 min. ▪ **TOTAL TIME:** 5 min.

½   cup sorghum syrup
½   cup malt or apple cider vinegar
3   Tbsp. bourbon
2   tsp. grated onion
1   tsp. salt
1   tsp. freshly ground black pepper
½   tsp. hot sauce
1   cup olive oil

Whisk together first 7 ingredients until blended. Add oil in a slow, steady stream, whisking until smooth.

LEMON BROCCOLINI

MAKES: 6 to 8 servings ▪ **HANDS-ON TIME:** 20 min. ▪ **TOTAL TIME:** 20 min.

1   cup (½-inch) French bread baguette cubes
2   Tbsp. butter
1   garlic clove, pressed
2   Tbsp. chopped fresh flat-leaf parsley
2   tsp. lemon zest
1½ lb. fresh Broccolini
2   Tbsp. fresh lemon juice
1   Tbsp. olive oil

1. Process bread in a food processor 30 seconds to 1 minute or until coarsely crumbled.

2. Melt butter with garlic in a large skillet over medium heat; add breadcrumbs, and cook, stirring constantly, 2 to 3 minutes or until golden brown. Remove from heat, and stir in parsley and lemon zest.

3. Cook Broccolini in boiling salted water to cover 3 to 4 minutes or until crisp-tender; drain well. Toss Broccolini with lemon juice and olive oil. Add salt and pepper to taste. Transfer to a serving platter, and sprinkle with breadcrumb mixture.

ASPARAGUS SAUTÉ

MAKES: 6 servings ▪ **HANDS-ON TIME:** 15 min. ▪ **TOTAL TIME:** 15 min.

2   lb. fresh asparagus
¼   cup butter
1   large red bell pepper, diced
½   tsp. table salt
½   tsp. freshly ground black pepper

1. Snap off and discard tough ends of asparagus. Cut asparagus into 2-inch pieces.

2. Melt butter in a large skillet over medium heat. Add asparagus, bell pepper, and remaining ingredients; sauté 4 to 5 minutes or until crisp-tender. Serve immediately.

PLAN AHEAD

This dish comes together quickly when you prepare the asparagus and chop the red bell pepper the night before.

LEMON BROCCOLINI

BALSAMIC GREEN BEANS

MAKES: 8 to 10 servings ▪ **HANDS-ON TIME:** 30 min. ▪ **TOTAL TIME:** 30 min.

2 lb. fresh haricots verts (thin green beans), trimmed*
6 large shallots
Vegetable oil
½ cup balsamic vinegar
1 Tbsp. light brown sugar
3 Tbsp. butter
½ cup lightly salted roasted almonds, coarsely chopped
½ cup cooked and crumbled bacon (about 5 slices)

1. Cook beans in boiling salted water to cover 3 to 4 minutes or until crisp-tender; drain. Plunge beans into ice water to stop cooking process; drain.
2. Cut shallots crosswise into thin slices; separate into rings. Pour oil to depth of 1 inch into a heavy saucepan; heat over medium-high heat to 350°. Fry shallots, in batches, 1 to 2 minutes or until crisp. Remove from skillet using a slotted spoon; drain on paper towels.
3. Cook vinegar and sugar in a large skillet over medium-high heat, stirring often, 5 to 6 minutes or until reduced to 3 Tbsp. Stir in butter until blended. Add beans, and sauté 5 minutes or until thoroughly heated; add salt and pepper to taste. Arrange on a serving platter. Top with shallots, almonds, and bacon. Serve immediately.

*Regular fresh green beans may be substituted. (You'll need to cook a few minutes longer.)

GREEN BEAN-GOAT CHEESE GRATIN

MAKES: 4 servings ▪ **HANDS-ON TIME:** 20 min. ▪ **TOTAL TIME:** 50 min.

2   *white bread slices*

1   *Tbsp. olive oil*

¾   *cup (3 oz.) freshly shredded Parmesan cheese, divided*

⅓   *cup finely chopped pecans*

1   *lb. fresh haricots verts (thin green beans), trimmed*

2   *oz. goat cheese, crumbled*

½   *cup whipping cream*

¼   *tsp. kosher salt*

¼   *tsp. freshly ground black pepper*

1. Preheat oven to 400°. Tear bread into large pieces; pulse in a food processor 2 or 3 times or until coarse crumbs form. Drizzle oil over crumbs; add ¼ cup Parmesan cheese. Pulse 5 or 6 times or until coated with oil. Stir in pecans.

2. Cut green beans crosswise into thirds. Cook in boiling water to cover 3 to 4 minutes or until crisp-tender; drain. Plunge into ice water to stop cooking process; drain and pat dry with paper towels.

3. Toss together beans, next 4 ingredients, and remaining ½ cup Parmesan cheese. Firmly pack mixture into 4 (6-oz.) shallow ramekins. Cover each with aluminum foil, and place on a baking sheet.

4. Bake at 400° for 20 minutes. Uncover and sprinkle with crumb mixture. Bake 8 more minutes or until golden. Let stand 5 minutes.

HOLIDAY TRADITION

Host a Christmas dinner and have each guest bring a favorite side dish or special family recipe that reminds them of a Christmas past. Green bean casseroles are a classic in the South. Bread slices, haricots verts, and crumbled goat cheese give this recipe an updated twist.

FRIED CONFETTI CORN

GREEN BEANS WITH
CARAMELIZED SHALLOTS

FRIED CONFETTI CORN

MAKES: 8 servings ▪ **HANDS-ON TIME:** 30 min. ▪ **TOTAL TIME:** 30 min.

8   bacon slices
6   cups fresh sweet corn kernels
      (about 8 ears)
1   cup diced sweet onion
½   cup chopped red bell pepper
½   cup chopped green bell pepper
1   (8-oz.) package cream cheese,
      cubed
½   cup half-and-half
1   tsp. sugar
1   tsp. table salt
1   tsp. freshly ground black pepper

1. Cook bacon in a large skillet over medium-high heat 6 to 8 minutes or until crisp. Remove bacon, and drain on paper towels, reserving 2 Tbsp. drippings in skillet. Coarsely crumble bacon.

2. Sauté corn and next 3 ingredients in hot drippings in skillet over medium-high heat 6 minutes or until tender. Add cream cheese and half-and-half, stirring until cream cheese melts. Stir in sugar and next 2 ingredients. Transfer to a serving dish, and top with bacon.

GREEN BEANS
with Caramelized Shallots

MAKES: 8 servings ▪ **HANDS-ON TIME:** 20 min. ▪ **TOTAL TIME:** 30 min.

2   lb. haricots verts (thin green
      beans), trimmed
3   Tbsp. butter
1   Tbsp. light brown sugar
1   Tbsp. olive oil
1   lb. shallots, halved lengthwise
      and peeled
2   Tbsp. red wine vinegar

1. Cook green beans in boiling salted water to cover 3 to 4 minutes or until crisp-tender; drain. Plunge beans into ice water to stop the cooking process; drain.

2. Melt butter and brown sugar with olive oil in a large skillet over medium-high heat; add shallots, and sauté 2 minutes. Reduce heat to medium-low, add vinegar, and sauté 10 minutes or until shallots are golden brown and tender.

3. Increase heat to medium-high; add green beans, and sauté 5 minutes or until thoroughly heated. Season with salt and freshly ground pepper to taste.

BALSAMIC-ROASTED CARROTS AND PARSNIPS

MAKES: 8 to 10 servings ▪ **HANDS-ON TIME:** 20 min. ▪ **TOTAL TIME:** 1 hour

1   (4-oz.) package feta cheese, crumbled
½   cup chopped dried sweet cherries
¼   cup chopped fresh flat-leaf parsley
1   tsp. lemon zest
½   tsp. dried crushed red pepper
4   Tbsp. olive oil, divided
1½ lb. carrots
1½ lb. parsnips
2   Tbsp. light brown sugar
1   Tbsp. balsamic vinegar

1. Preheat oven to 400°. Toss together first 5 ingredients and 1 Tbsp. olive oil in a small bowl.

2. Cut carrots and parsnips lengthwise into long, thin strips.

3. Whisk together brown sugar, balsamic vinegar, and remaining 3 Tbsp. olive oil in a large bowl. Toss with carrots and parsnips, and place on a lightly greased 15- x 10-inch jelly-roll pan. Add salt and pepper to taste.

4. Bake at 400° for 40 to 45 minutes or until vegetables are tender and browned, stirring every 15 minutes. Transfer to a serving platter, and gently toss with feta cheese mixture.

CRANBERRY ROASTED
WINTER VEGETABLES

CRANBERRY ROASTED WINTER VEGETABLES

MAKES: 8 servings ▪ **HANDS-ON TIME:** 30 min. ▪ **TOTAL TIME:** 1 hour, 5 min.

4   large carrots (about 1 ½ lb.),
      halved lengthwise and cut into
      1-inch pieces
3   large turnips (about 2 lb.),
      peeled and cut into 1-inch pieces*
1   lb. Brussels sprouts, halved
      (quartered, if large)
1   Tbsp. minced fresh rosemary
2   Tbsp. olive oil
¾   tsp. table salt
¼   tsp. freshly ground black pepper
1   cup fresh or thawed frozen
      cranberries
4   tsp. molasses

1. Preheat oven to 400°. Lightly grease 2 large jelly-roll pans; place carrots and turnips in one pan and Brussels sprouts in second pan. Divide rosemary and next 3 ingredients between carrot mixture and Brussels sprouts; toss each to coat.

2. Bake both pans at 400° at same time. Bake carrot mixture 30 minutes, stirring once; add cranberries, and bake 5 more minutes or until carrots and turnips are tender and browned and cranberries begin to soften. Bake Brussels sprouts 15 to 20 minutes or until tender and browned, stirring once.

3. Remove vegetables from oven, and combine in a large serving bowl. Drizzle with molasses, and toss to coat.

2 lb. parsnips may be substituted.

ORANGE-GLAZED SWEET POTATOES

MAKES: 8 servings ▪ **HANDS-ON TIME:** 15 min. ▪ **TOTAL TIME:** 1 hour, 5 min.

6   medium-size sweet potatoes
      (about 4 lb.)
¼   cup firmly packed dark
      brown sugar
½   tsp. orange zest
1   cup fresh orange juice
2   Tbsp. butter, melted
¼   tsp. kosher salt
¼   tsp. ground cinnamon

1. Preheat oven to 325°. Peel potatoes, and cut into 1-inch-thick slices; arrange in a single layer in 2 lightly greased 13-x 9-inch baking dishes.

2. Stir together brown sugar and next 5 ingredients; pour over potatoes. Cover with aluminum foil.

3. Bake at 325° for 45 minutes or until fork-tender. Uncover and bake 5 more minutes or until glaze becomes syrupy.

***Make Ahead:** Cover and chill cooked potatoes up to 1 day. To reheat, let stand at room temperature 1 hour. Bake, uncovered, at 350° for 20 minutes.*

SWEET POTATO-CARROT CASSEROLE

MAKES: 8 to 10 servings ▪ **HANDS-ON TIME:** 40 min. ▪ **TOTAL TIME:** 3 hours, 40 min.

6   *large sweet potatoes (about 5 lb.)*
1½ *lb. carrots, sliced*
¼   *cup butter*
1   *cup sour cream*
2   *Tbsp. sugar*
1   *tsp. lemon zest*
½   *tsp. ground nutmeg*
½   *tsp. table salt*
½   *tsp. freshly ground black pepper*
1½ *cups miniature marshmallows*
1   *cup Sugar-and-Spice Pecans*

1. Preheat oven to 400°. Bake sweet potatoes on an aluminum foil-lined 15- x 10-inch jelly-roll pan 1 hour or until tender. Reduce oven temperature to 350°. Cool potatoes 30 minutes.

2. Meanwhile, cook carrots in boiling water to cover 20 to 25 minutes or until very tender; drain.

3. Process carrots and butter in a food processor until smooth, stopping to scrape down sides as needed. Transfer carrot mixture to a large bowl.

4. Peel and cube sweet potatoes. Process, in batches, in food processor until smooth, stopping to scrape down sides as needed. Add sweet potatoes to carrot mixture. Stir in sour cream and next 5 ingredients, stirring until blended. Spoon mixture into a lightly greased 13- x 9-inch baking dish.

5. Bake at 350° for 30 minutes or until thoroughly heated. Remove from oven. Sprinkle with marshmallows. Bake 10 more minutes or until marshmallows are golden brown. Remove from oven, and sprinkle with Sugar-and-Spice Pecans.

Make Ahead: *Prepare recipe as directed through Step 4; cover and chill up to 24 hours. Remove from refrigerator, and let stand 30 minutes. Proceed with recipe as directed in Step 5.*

Sugar-and-Spice Pecans

MAKES: 4 cups ▪ **HANDS-ON TIME:** 15 min. ▪ **TOTAL TIME:** 1 hour, 10 min.

1   *egg white*
4   *cups pecan halves and pieces*
½   *cup sugar*
1   *Tbsp. orange zest*
1   *tsp. ground cinnamon*
1   *tsp. ground ginger*

1. Preheat oven to 350°. Whisk egg white in a large bowl until foamy. Add pecans, and stir until evenly coated.

2. Stir together sugar and next 3 ingredients in a small bowl until blended. Sprinkle sugar mixture over pecans; stir gently until pecans are evenly coated. Spread pecans in a single layer in a lightly greased aluminum foil-lined 15- x 10-inch jelly-roll pan.

3. Bake at 350° for 24 to 26 minutes or until pecans are toasted and dry, stirring once after 10 minutes. Remove from oven, and cool completely (about 30 minutes).

Make Ahead: *Prepare pecans as directed. Store in a zip-top plastic freezer bag at room temperature up to 3 days, or freeze up to 3 weeks.*

CREAMY SPINACH
MASHED POTATO BAKE

CARAMELIZED ONION
MASHED POTATO BAKE

SMOKY SWEET POTATO
MASHED POTATO BAKE

BACON-AND
BLUE CHEESE
MASHED POTAT
BAKE

TASTY TEX-MEX
MASHED POTATO
BAKE

BUTTERMILK MASHED POTATOES

MAKES: 6 to 8 servings ▪ **HANDS-ON TIME:** 25 min. ▪ **TOTAL TIME:** 50 min.

4   lb. baking potatoes, peeled
     and cut into 2-inch pieces
3   tsp. table salt, divided
¾   cup warm buttermilk
½   cup warm milk
¼   cup butter, melted
½   tsp. freshly ground black pepper

1. Bring potatoes, 2 tsp. salt, and water to cover to a boil in a large Dutch oven over medium-high heat; boil 20 minutes or until tender. Drain. Reduce heat to low. Return potatoes to Dutch oven, and cook, stirring occasionally, 3 to 5 minutes or until potatoes are dry.

2. Mash potatoes with a potato masher to desired consistency. Stir in buttermilk, milk, butter, black pepper, and remaining 1 tsp. salt, stirring just until blended.

Try these twists!

Prepare Buttermilk Mashed Potatoes as directed, increasing buttermilk to 1¼ cups. Stir in one of the tasty combos below, and spoon the mixture into a lightly greased 2½-qt. baking dish or 8 (10-oz.) ramekins. Bake at 350° for 35 minutes.

Smoky Sweet Potato Mashed Potato Bake: 1 cup mashed baked sweet potatoes and 1½ Tbsp. chopped canned chipotle peppers in adobo sauce

Creamy Spinach Mashed Potato Bake: 1 (5-oz.) package fresh baby spinach, wilted; 1 (5½-oz.) package buttery garlic-and-herb spreadable cheese; and ¼ cup chopped toasted pecans

Caramelized Onion Mashed Potato Bake: 1¼ cups freshly grated Gruyère cheese, 1 cup chopped caramelized onions, and 2 Tbsp. chopped fresh parsley

Bacon-and-Blue Cheese Mashed Potato Bake: 1 (4-oz.) wedge blue cheese, crumbled, and 8 cooked and crumbled bacon slices

Tasty Tex-Mex Mashed Potato Bake: 1 (4.5-oz.) can chopped green chiles, 1¼ cups (5 oz.) shredded pepper Jack cheese, and ½ cup finely chopped cooked chorizo sausage

FENNEL-AND-POTATO GRATIN

MAKES: 8 servings ▪ **HANDS-ON TIME:** 30 min. ▪ **TOTAL TIME:** 1 hour, 22 min.

3   Tbsp. butter
1   shallot, sliced
1   garlic clove, minced
2   Tbsp. all-purpose flour
1¼ cups half-and-half
½   (10-oz.) block sharp white
      Cheddar cheese, shredded
½   tsp. table salt
¼   tsp. freshly ground black pepper
⅛   tsp. ground nutmeg
2   large baking potatoes
      (about 2 lb.), peeled and thinly
      sliced
1   small fennel bulb, thinly sliced
Garnish: fresh rosemary sprigs

1. Preheat oven to 400°. Melt butter in a heavy saucepan over medium heat. Add shallot and sauté 2 to 3 minutes or until tender. Add garlic, and sauté 1 minute.

2. Whisk in flour; cook, whisking constantly, 1 minute. Gradually whisk in half-and-half, and cook, whisking constantly, 3 to 4 minutes or until thickened and bubbly. Remove from heat. Whisk in cheese until melted and smooth. Stir in salt and next 2 ingredients.

3. Layer potato and fennel slices alternately in a lightly greased, broiler-safe 2-qt. baking dish. Spread cheese sauce over layers. Cover with aluminum foil.

4. Bake at 400° for 50 minutes or until potatoes are tender. Remove from oven. Increase oven temperature to broil with oven rack 5 inches from heat. Uncover and broil 2 to 4 minutes or until golden brown.

WRAP IT UP

Potted rosemary, the sign of love and friendship, makes the perfect Christmas gift. Wrap the pot in burlap, tie with ribbon, and attach a favorite holiday recipe or two that uses the fragrant herb, including this recipe.

BUTTERNUT SQUASH GRATIN

MAKES: 8 servings ▪ **HANDS-ON TIME:** 45 min. ▪ **TOTAL TIME:** 3 hours, 30 min.

1   (3-lb.) butternut squash
1   (3-lb.) spaghetti squash
2   Tbsp. butter, melted
1   cup firmly packed light brown
      sugar, divided
½   tsp. ground cinnamon
¼   tsp. ground nutmeg
3   cups whipping cream
5   large Yukon gold potatoes
      (about 2½ lb.)
1   tsp. table salt
1   tsp. freshly ground black pepper
4   cups (16 oz.) freshly shredded
      fontina cheese*

Garnish: fresh rosemary sprigs

*Gouda cheese may be substituted.

Tip: To help prevent the potatoes from turning brown (oxidizing), slice them as you use them in each layer, rather than all at once.

1. Preheat oven to 450°. Cut butternut and spaghetti squash in half lengthwise; remove and discard seeds. Place squash, cut sides up, in a lightly greased 17- x 12-inch jelly-roll pan. Drizzle with butter, and sprinkle with ½ cup brown sugar. Bake at 450° for 40 minutes or until tender. Cool 20 minutes.

2. Using a fork, scrape inside of spaghetti squash to remove spaghetti-like strands, and place in a large bowl. Scoop pulp from butternut squash; coarsely chop pulp, and toss with spaghetti squash.

3. Stir together cinnamon, nutmeg, and remaining ½ cup brown sugar.

4. Cook cream in a heavy nonaluminum saucepan over medium heat, stirring often, 5 minutes or just until it begins to steam (do not boil); remove from heat.

5. Using a mandoline or sharp knife, cut potatoes into ⅛-inch-thick slices.

6. Arrange one-fourth of potato slices in a thin layer on bottom of a greased 13- x 9-inch baking dish. Spoon one-third of squash mixture over potatoes (squash layer should be about ¼ inch thick); sprinkle with ¼ tsp. salt, ¼ tsp. black pepper, 1 cup fontina cheese, and ¾ cup hot cream. Repeat layers twice, sprinkling one-third of sugar mixture over each of second and third squash layers. (Do not sprinkle sugar mixture over first squash layer.) Top with remaining potato slices, ¼ tsp. salt, and ¼ tsp. black pepper. Gently press layers down with back of a spoon. Sprinkle top with remaining 1 cup cheese and ¾ cup hot cream; sprinkle with remaining brown sugar mixture. Place baking dish on an aluminum foil-lined baking sheet.

7. Bake, covered with foil, at 450° for 1 hour; uncover and bake 25 more minutes or until golden brown and potatoes are tender. Cool on a wire rack 20 minutes before serving.

SQUASH CASSEROLE

MAKES: 8 to 10 servings ▪ **HANDS-ON TIME:** 40 min. ▪ **TOTAL TIME:** 1 hour, 15 min.

4   lb. yellow squash, sliced
1   large sweet onion, finely chopped
1   cup (4 oz.) freshly shredded
      Cheddar cheese
2   large eggs, lightly beaten
1   cup mayonnaise
2   Tbsp. chopped fresh basil
1   tsp. garlic salt
1   tsp. freshly ground black pepper
2   cups soft, fresh breadcrumbs,
      divided
1¼ cups (5 oz.) freshly shredded
      Parmesan cheese, divided
2   Tbsp. butter, melted
½   cup crushed French fried onions

1. Preheat oven to 350°. Cook squash and sweet onion in boiling water to cover in a Dutch oven 8 minutes or just until vegetables are tender; drain squash mixture well.

2. Combine squash mixture, freshly shredded Cheddar cheese, next 5 ingredients, 1 cup breadcrumbs, and ¾ cup Parmesan cheese. Spoon into a lightly greased 13- x 9-inch baking dish.

3. Stir together melted butter, French fried onions, and remaining 1 cup breadcrumbs and ½ cup Parmesan cheese. Sprinkle over squash mixture.

4. Bake at 350° for 35 to 40 minutes or until set, shielding with aluminum foil after 20 to 25 minutes to prevent excessive browning, if necessary. Let stand 10 minutes before serving.

Fresh squash and basil, a mix of Parmesan and Cheddar cheeses, and a crunchy breadcrumb topping all make this squash casserole divine.

FOUR-CHEESE MACARONI

MAKES: 8 servings ▪ **HANDS-ON TIME:** 40 min. ▪ **TOTAL TIME:** 1 hour, 15 min.

12 oz. cavatappi pasta
½ cup butter
½ cup all-purpose flour
½ tsp. ground red pepper
3 cups milk
2 cups (8 oz.) freshly shredded
    white Cheddar cheese
1 cup (4 oz.) freshly shredded
    Monterey Jack cheese
1 cup (4 oz.) freshly shredded
    fontina cheese
1 cup (4 oz.) freshly shredded
    Asiago cheese
1½ cups soft, fresh breadcrumbs
½ cup chopped cooked bacon
½ cup chopped pecans
2 Tbsp. butter, melted

1. Preheat oven to 350°. Prepare pasta according to package directions.

2. Meanwhile, melt ½ cup butter in a Dutch oven over low heat; whisk in flour and ground red pepper until smooth. Cook, whisking constantly, 1 minute. Gradually whisk in milk; cook over medium heat, whisking constantly, 6 to 7 minutes or until milk mixture is thickened and bubbly. Remove from heat.

3. Toss together Cheddar cheese and next 3 ingredients in a medium bowl; reserve 1½ cups cheese mixture. Add remaining cheese mixture and hot cooked pasta to sauce, tossing to coat. Spoon into a lightly greased 13- x 9-inch baking dish. Top with reserved 1½ cups cheese mixture.

4. Toss together breadcrumbs and next 3 ingredients; sprinkle over cheese mixture.

5. Bake at 350° for 35 to 40 minutes or until bubbly and golden brown.

HOLIDAY TRADITION

Hosting families with children can be a fun way to celebrate the season, but cooking separate dishes for adults and kids can be tiring. Serve a side such as this macaroni and cheese that the entire party will enjoy.

WILD RICE
with Bacon and Fennel

MAKES: 8 servings ▪ HANDS-ON TIME: 40 min. ▪ TOTAL TIME: 1 hour, 5 min.

1⅓ cups uncooked wild rice
4 bacon slices
1 large fennel bulb, thinly sliced
1 large onion, cut into thin wedges
2 garlic cloves, minced
½ cup reduced-sodium fat-free
   chicken broth
⅓ cup golden raisins
¼ tsp. table salt
⅛ tsp. freshly ground black pepper
¼ cup chopped fresh fennel
   fronds or flat-leaf parsley
1 Tbsp. white wine vinegar
½ cup chopped toasted walnuts

1. Cook wild rice according to package directions; drain.
2. Meanwhile, cook bacon in a large nonstick skillet over medium-high heat 7 to 8 minutes or until crisp; remove bacon, and drain on paper towels, reserving 1 Tbsp. drippings in skillet. Chop bacon.
3. Sauté fennel bulb and onion in hot drippings over medium-high heat 5 minutes or until softened. Add garlic; sauté 1 minute. Add broth and next 3 ingredients; bring to a boil. Reduce heat to medium-low; cover and simmer 8 minutes or until vegetables are tender. Stir in rice and bacon; cook, stirring often, 3 minutes.
4. Transfer to a large serving bowl. Stir in fennel fronds and vinegar. Stir in walnuts just before serving.

Tip: *For the best texture, use wild rice, not a blend.*

WILD RICE
with Mushrooms

MAKES: 8 to 10 servings ▪ HANDS-ON TIME: 30 min. ▪ TOTAL TIME: 30 min.

2 (6-oz.) packages long-grain and
   wild rice mix
3 Tbsp. butter
1 large sweet onion, diced
12 oz. assorted fresh mushrooms,
   trimmed and sliced
¼ tsp. table salt
½ cup Marsala
½ cup chopped fresh flat-leaf
   parsley

1. Cook rice mix according to package directions.
2. Meanwhile, melt butter in a large skillet over medium-high heat; add onion, and sauté 7 minutes or until golden. Add mushrooms and salt; sauté 4 to 5 minutes or until mushrooms are tender. Add Marsala, and sauté 3 minutes or until liquid is absorbed. Stir mushroom mixture and parsley into prepared rice.

WILD RICE WITH BACON
AND FENNEL

CREOLE CORNBREAD DRESSING

MAKES: 14 to 16 servings ▪ **HANDS-ON TIME:** 55 min. ▪ **TOTAL TIME:** 2 hours, 55 min.

1 (12-oz.) package andouille sausage, chopped
8 green onions, thinly sliced
3 large celery ribs, diced
1 large sweet onion, diced
1 medium-size green bell pepper, diced
Cornbread Crumbles
½ cup butter
1 (8-oz.) package fresh mushrooms, diced
1 cup dry sherry
½ cup chopped fresh parsley
2 cups chopped toasted pecans
2 Tbsp. Creole seasoning
2 (14-oz.) cans reduced-sodium fat-free chicken broth
2 large eggs

1. Preheat oven to 350°. Sauté andouille sausage in a large skillet over medium-high heat 3 to 4 minutes or until lightly browned. Add green onions and next 3 ingredients, and sauté 5 minutes or until vegetables are tender. Transfer mixture to a large bowl; stir in Cornbread Crumbles.
2. Melt butter in skillet over medium-high heat; add mushrooms, and sauté 3 minutes. Add sherry, and cook, stirring often, 5 to 6 minutes or until liquid is reduced by half; stir in parsley. Stir mushroom mixture, toasted pecans, and Creole seasoning into cornbread mixture.
3. Whisk together chicken broth and eggs; add to cornbread mixture, stirring gently just until moistened. Divide mixture between 1 lightly greased 13- x 9-inch baking dish and 1 lightly greased 8-inch square baking dish.
4. Bake at 350° for 40 to 45 minutes or until golden brown.

Cornbread Crumbles

MAKES: 1 dressing recipe ▪ **HANDS-ON TIME:** 10 min. ▪ **TOTAL TIME:** 1 hour, 10 min.

3 cups self-rising white cornmeal mix
1 cup all-purpose flour
2 Tbsp. sugar
3 cups buttermilk
3 large eggs, lightly beaten
½ cup butter, melted

Preheat oven to 425°. Stir together first 3 ingredients in a large bowl; whisk in buttermilk, eggs, and butter. Pour batter into a lightly greased 13- x 9-inch pan. Bake at 425° for 30 minutes or until golden brown. Remove from oven, invert onto a wire rack, and cool completely (about 30 minutes); crumble cornbread.

FESTIVE MAIN DISHES

Gather around the table to celebrate this year's blessings with one of these entrées. Make our creamy chicken casserole, glazed ham, or grilled turkey the star of your holiday meal.

PANCETTA-AND-FIG PASTA

Bucatini is a hearty, hollow, spaghetti-like pasta. You can substitute linguine or fettuccine, if you prefer.

MAKES: 6 servings ▪ **HANDS-ON TIME:** 25 min. ▪ **TOTAL TIME:** 35 min.

1   (16-oz.) package bucatini pasta
5   oz. thinly sliced pancetta, chopped (about 1 cup)
2   shallots, minced
1   garlic clove, minced
¾   cup heavy cream
½   cup freshly grated Parmesan cheese
12   fresh figs, quartered
⅓   cup torn basil leaves

1. Cook pasta in boiling salted water according to package directions; drain, reserving 1 cup hot pasta water.
2. Sauté pancetta, shallots, and garlic in a large skillet over medium heat 6 to 7 minutes or until pancetta is golden and shallots are tender. Add cream, cheese, and hot cooked pasta; cook, stirring constantly, 2 to 3 minutes or until cheese melts. Stir in ¾ to 1 cup reserved pasta water until creamy. Add salt and pepper to taste. Transfer to a serving dish. Sprinkle with figs and basil. Serve immediately.

BUTTERNUT SQUASH RAVIOLI WITH MUSHROOMS

MAKES: 8 servings ▪ **HANDS-ON TIME:** 25 min. ▪ **TOTAL TIME:** 25 min.

2   (8-oz.) packages refrigerated butternut squash-filled ravioli
6   Tbsp. butter, divided
1   (8-oz.) package sliced baby portobello mushrooms
4   garlic cloves, thinly sliced
3   Tbsp. sliced fresh shallots
2   Tbsp. chopped fresh flat-leaf parsley
1   Tbsp. thinly sliced fresh sage
1   tsp. kosher salt
¼   tsp. black pepper
Toppings: freshly shaved Parmesan cheese, black pepper, chopped fresh parsley

1. Prepare butternut squash-filled ravioli according to package directions. Keep warm.
2. Melt 2 Tbsp. butter in a large skillet over medium heat. Add mushrooms; sauté 3 to 5 minutes or until lightly browned. Add garlic and shallots; sauté 2 minutes or until tender. Remove from skillet. Wipe skillet clean.
3. Melt remaining 4 Tbsp. butter in skillet over medium heat; cook 2 to 3 minutes or until lightly browned. Stir in parsley, sage, and mushroom mixture. Add hot cooked ravioli, and toss gently. Stir in salt and black pepper. Serve immediately with desired toppings.

Note: *We tested with Whole Foods 365 Everyday Value Butternut Squash Ravioli.*

ROQUEFORT NOODLES

Don't skimp on the quality of the blue cheese in this recipe.

MAKES: 6 to 8 servings ▪ **HANDS-ON TIME:** 20 min. ▪ **TOTAL TIME:** 20 min.

1   *(12-oz.) package wide egg
      noodles*
1   *Tbsp. jarred chicken soup base*
½   *tsp. olive oil*
½   *cup butter*
6   *to 8 green onions, sliced*
4   *to 6 oz. Roquefort or other blue
      cheese, crumbled*
1   *(8-oz.) container sour cream*

1. Cook egg noodles according to package directions, adding chicken soup base and oil to water.

2. Meanwhile, melt butter in a large heavy skillet over medium heat. Add onions, and sauté 5 to 7 minutes or until tender. Reduce heat to medium-low, and stir in Roquefort cheese, stirring constantly, until cheese is melted. Remove from heat, and stir in sour cream until blended and smooth.

3. Toss together Roquefort cheese sauce and hot cooked egg noodles. Add pepper to taste.

Note: *We tested with Superior Touch Better Than Bouillon Chicken Base.*

HOLIDAY TRADITION

Enjoy more time with the family and less time in the kitchen with this quick 20-minute dish. End the evening around the tree with store-bought cookies and hot cocoa.

CARAMELIZED MAPLE-AND-GARLIC-GLAZED SALMON

MAKES: 8 servings ▪ **HANDS-ON TIME:** 20 min. ▪ **TOTAL TIME:** 20 min.

8 (2-inch-thick) salmon fillets
   (about 2½ lb.)
¾ tsp. table salt
¾ tsp. garlic powder
2 Tbsp. butter
⅓ cup maple syrup, divided
1 Tbsp. chopped fresh chives

1. Preheat broiler with oven rack 5½ inches from heat. Sprinkle salmon with salt and garlic powder.

2. Melt butter in a large skillet over medium heat. Add salmon, skin side up; cook 2 minutes. Place salmon, skin side down, on a lightly greased rack in a broiler pan; brush with half of syrup.

3. Broil salmon 5 to 7 minutes or until fish reaches desired degree of doneness and syrup begins to caramelize. Brush with remaining syrup; sprinkle with chives.

Maple syrup isn't just for pancakes. When brushed on salmon and broiled, maple syrup delivers a succulent flavor in this delicious main dish.

CREAMY CHICKEN-AND-WILD RICE CASSEROLE

MAKES: 10 to 12 servings ▪ **HANDS-ON TIME:** 30 min. ▪ **TOTAL TIME:** 1 hour, 10 min.

2   (6.2-oz.) boxes fast-cooking
      long-grain and wild rice mix
¼   cup butter
4   celery ribs, chopped
2   medium onions, chopped
5   cups chopped cooked chicken
2   (10¾-oz.) cans cream of
      mushroom soup
2   (8-oz.) cans chopped water
      chestnuts, drained
1   (8-oz.) container sour cream
1   cup milk
½   tsp. table salt
½   tsp. black pepper
4   cups (16 oz.) shredded Cheddar
      cheese, divided
2   cups soft fresh breadcrumbs
1   (2.25-oz.) package sliced
      almonds, toasted

1. Prepare rice mixes according to package directions.

2. Meanwhile, melt butter in a large skillet over medium heat; add celery and onions. Sauté 10 minutes or until tender.

3. Preheat oven to 350°. Stir in chicken, next 6 ingredients, rice, and 3 cups cheese. Spoon mixture into a lightly greased 15- x 10-inch baking dish or 2 (11- x 7-inch) baking dishes. Top casserole with breadcrumbs.

4. Bake, uncovered, at 350° for 35 minutes. Sprinkle with remaining 1 cup cheese; top with toasted almonds. Bake 5 more minutes.

__Make Ahead:__ Prepare recipe as directed through Step 3. Cover with aluminum foil, and freeze up to 1 month. Remove from freezer, and let stand at room temperature 1 hour. Bake, covered, at 350° for 30 minutes. Uncover casserole, and bake 1 hour and 15 more minutes. Sprinkle with 1 cup (4 oz.) shredded Cheddar cheese, and top with toasted almonds; bake 5 more minutes.

Try these twists!

Prepare Creamy Chicken-and-Wild Rice Casserole as directed, making the following substitutions.

Shrimp-and-Wild Rice Casserole: Substitute 2 lb. peeled and deveined medium-size raw shrimp for chicken, 2 cups (8 oz.) shredded Monterey Jack cheese and 2 cups grated Parmesan cheese for Cheddar cheese, and 1 cup dry white wine for milk.

Cajun Chicken-and-Wild Rice Casserole: Omit salt and pepper. Reduce chicken to 2½ cups. Prepare as directed, sautéing 1 lb. andouille sausage, chopped, and 1 green bell pepper, diced, with celery in Step 3. Stir 1 (15-oz.) can black-eyed peas, drained, and 1 tsp. Cajun seasoning into rice mixture. Proceed as directed.

SKILLET CHICKEN POT PIE

MAKES: 6 to 8 servings ▪ **HANDS-ON TIME:** 30 min. ▪ **TOTAL TIME:** 1 hour, 30 min.

CHICKEN PIE FILLING

⅓ cup butter
⅓ cup all-purpose flour
1½ cups chicken broth
1½ cups milk
1½ tsp. Creole seasoning
2 Tbsp. butter
1 large sweet onion, diced
1 (8-oz.) package sliced fresh
   mushrooms
4 cups shredded cooked chicken
2 cups frozen cubed hash browns
1 cup matchstick carrots
1 cup frozen small sweet peas
⅓ cup chopped fresh parsley

PASTRY CRUST

1 (14.1-oz.) package refrigerated
   piecrusts
1 egg white

1. Prepare Filling: Preheat oven to 350°. Melt ⅓ cup butter in a large saucepan over medium heat; add all-purpose flour, and cook, whisking constantly, 1 minute. Gradually add chicken broth and milk, and cook, whisking constantly, 6 to 7 minutes or until thickened and bubbly. Remove from heat, and stir in Creole seasoning.

2. Melt 2 Tbsp. butter in a large Dutch oven over medium-high heat; add onion and mushrooms, and sauté 10 minutes or until tender. Stir in chicken, next 4 ingredients, and sauce.

3. Prepare Crust: Place 1 piecrust in a lightly greased 10-inch cast-iron skillet. Spoon chicken mixture over piecrust, and top with remaining piecrust.

4. Whisk egg white until foamy; brush top of piecrust with egg white. Cut 4 to 5 slits in top of pie for steam to escape.

5. Bake at 350° for 1 hour to 1 hour and 5 minutes or until golden brown and bubbly.

ROASTED CHICKEN

MAKES: 4 to 6 servings ▪ **HANDS-ON TIME:** 20 min. ▪ **TOTAL TIME:** 1 hour, 35 min.

1   (4- to 5-lb.) whole chicken
1½ tsp. kosher salt, divided
1   lemon half
1   tsp. seasoned black pepper
1   tsp. dried rosemary
1   Tbsp. olive oil
1   Tbsp. butter, melted
Garnishes: fresh rosemary,
       lemon wedges

1. Preheat oven to 450°. If applicable, remove neck and giblets from chicken, and reserve for another use. Rinse chicken with cold water, and drain cavity well. Pat dry with paper towels. Sprinkle ½ tsp. salt inside cavity. Place lemon half inside cavity.
2. Stir together black pepper, rosemary, and remaining 1 tsp. salt. Brush outside of chicken with oil. Rub 2½ tsp. pepper mixture into skin. Sprinkle remaining pepper mixture over both sides of breast. Place chicken, breast side up, on a lightly greased wire rack in a lightly greased shallow roasting pan. Add ¾ cup water to pan.
3. Bake at 450° for 20 minutes. Reduce oven temperature to 375°, and bake 30 minutes. Baste chicken with pan juices; drizzle with melted butter. Bake 15 to 25 more minutes or until a meat thermometer inserted into thickest portion of thigh registers 165°, shielding with aluminum foil after 8 to 12 minutes to prevent excessive browning, if necessary. Remove chicken from oven, and baste with pan juices. Let stand 10 minutes before slicing.

Note: *We tested with McCormick Gourmet Collection Crushed Rosemary.*

ROASTED PAPRIKA CHICKEN

MAKES: 6 to 8 servings ▪ **HANDS-ON TIME:** 20 min. ▪ **TOTAL TIME:** 1 hour

¼   cup smoked paprika
2   Tbsp. chopped fresh thyme
3   Tbsp. extra virgin olive oil
2   tsp. kosher salt
1   tsp. coarsely ground black
       pepper
5   lb. skin-on, bone-in chicken
       thighs and breasts
2   lemons, thinly sliced

1. Preheat oven to 425°. Stir together first 5 ingredients, forming a paste.
2. Loosen and lift skin from chicken pieces with fingers (do not totally detach skin). Spread half of paprika mixture underneath skin. Place lemon slices on paprika mixture under skin; carefully replace skin. Rub remaining paprika mixture evenly over outside of skin. Arrange chicken pieces in a single layer on a lightly greased wire rack in an aluminum foil-lined 18- x 12-inch jelly-roll pan.
3. Bake at 425° for 35 to 40 minutes or until a meat thermometer inserted into thickest portion of each piece registers 165°. Let chicken stand 5 minutes; lightly brush with pan juices just before serving.

ROASTED CHICKEN

ROASTED CHICKEN
with Sweet Potatoes and Apples

MAKES: 8 servings ▪ **HANDS-ON TIME:** 40 min. ▪ **TOTAL TIME:** 2 hours, 20 min.

1   lemon
½   cup butter, softened
2   garlic cloves, minced
1   tsp. kosher salt, divided
1   tsp. freshly ground black
     pepper, divided
1   (5- to 6-lb.) whole chicken
3   fresh thyme sprigs
Kitchen string
1   large sweet potato (about 1 lb.)
2   large Granny Smith apples
     (about 1 lb.)
4   Tbsp. cup firmly packed dark
     brown sugar
¼   cup butter, melted
Garnishes: lemon slices, fresh
     thyme sprigs

1. Preheat oven to 425°. Grate zest from lemon to equal 2 tsp; reserve lemon. Combine zest, softened butter, garlic, and ½ tsp. each salt and black pepper. If applicable, remove neck and giblets from chicken, and reserve for another use. Rinse chicken, and pat dry. Loosen and lift skin from chicken breast with fingers (do not totally detach skin); spread half of butter mixture underneath skin, and place thyme sprigs under skin. Carefully replace skin.

2. Cut reserved lemon in half. Squeeze lemon juice into cavity of chicken, and place lemon halves in cavity. Tie ends of legs together with string; tuck wing tips under. Rub remaining butter mixture over chicken, and sprinkle with remaining ½ tsp. each salt and black pepper. Place chicken, breast side up, on a lightly greased rack in a lightly greased large, shallow roasting pan.

3. Bake chicken at 425° for 30 minutes.

4. Meanwhile, peel sweet potato and apples. Cut potato in half lengthwise, and cut into ¼-inch-thick half-moon slices. Cut apples in half vertically through stem and bottom ends, and cut into ¼-inch-thick wedges. Arrange half of sweet potatoes in bottom of a 9-inch oval gratin dish. Sprinkle with 1 Tbsp. brown sugar. Arrange apple wedges in a single layer over sweet potatoes; sprinke with 1 Tbsp. brown sugar. Top with remaining sweet potatoes, and sprinkle with remaining 2 Tbsp. brown sugar; drizzle with ¼ cup melted butter. Add salt and pepper to taste.

5. Reduce oven temperature to 350°. Bake chicken 15 more minutes. Add potato mixture to oven, and bake chicken and potato mixture at same time for 35 minutes. Uncover potato mixture, and bake 40 more minutes or until a meat thermometer inserted into thickest portion of chicken thigh registers 180° and potatoes and apples are tender and lightly browned.

BAKED CHICKEN ROULADE

MAKES: 4 servings ■ **HANDS-ON TIME:** 30 min. ■ **TOTAL TIME:** 45 min.

4 skinned and boned chicken
    breasts (about 1½ lb.)
½ tsp. black pepper
¼ tsp. table salt
1 (5-oz.) package baby spinach
4 garlic cloves, minced and divided
2 tsp. olive oil
12 fresh thin asparagus spears
    (about 1 lb.)
Wooden picks
5 Tbsp. butter, divided
2 Tbsp. olive oil
1 Tbsp. all-purpose flour
2 Tbsp. dry white wine
¾ cup chicken broth
1 tsp. fresh lemon juice
2 Tbsp. chopped fresh flat-leaf
    parsley
2 Tbsp. drained capers

1. Preheat oven to 425°. Place chicken between 2 sheets of heavy-duty plastic wrap, and flatten to ¼-inch thickness using flat side of a meat mallet or rolling pin. Sprinkle chicken with black pepper and salt.

2. Sauté spinach and 2 minced garlic cloves in 2 tsp. hot oil in a large ovenproof skillet over medium heat 1 minute or until spinach begins to wilt. Transfer spinach mixture to a plate. Wipe skillet clean.

3. Spoon spinach mixture over each breast, leaving a ½-inch border around edges. Top with asparagus, and roll up, starting at 1 short side. Tuck in ends of chicken, and secure with wooden picks.

4. Melt 3 Tbsp. butter with 2 Tbsp. oil in skillet over medium-high heat; add chicken. Cook 6 to 8 minutes, turning to brown on all sides. Transfer skillet to oven, and bake at 425° for 15 minutes. Transfer to a serving plate, and cover loosely with aluminum foil to keep warm.

5. Melt remaining 2 Tbsp. butter in skillet over medium-high heat; add remaining garlic. Sauté 1 to 2 minutes or until tender and fragrant. Whisk in flour; cook 1 minute. Add white wine; cook, stirring constantly, 1 minute. Whisk in chicken broth and lemon juice; cook 2 minutes or until thickened. Stir in parsley and capers; spoon sauce over chicken, and serve immediately.

FIG-AND-BALSAMIC-GLAZED QUAIL

Call ahead to be sure your butcher has quail on hand. For a delicious alternative, use cornish hens. (See Fig-and-Balsamic-Glazed Cornish Hens below.)

MAKES: 8 servings ▪ **HANDS-ON TIME:** 20 min. ▪ **TOTAL TIME:** 1 hour, 15 min.

1   (11.5-oz.) jar fig preserves
½   cup dry red wine
3   Tbsp. balsamic vinegar
½   tsp. coarsely ground black
       pepper
2   tsp. country-style Dijon mustard
8   (3.5-oz.) semiboneless quail
Kitchen string
1   tsp. kosher salt
2   Tbsp. dry red wine

1. Preheat oven to 450°. Bring first 5 ingredients to a boil in a small saucepan over medium-high heat; reduce heat to low, and simmer 8 to 10 minutes or until slightly thickened. Reserve half of fig mixture; cover and chill. Let remaining fig mixture stand at room temperature.

2. Tie ends of quail legs together with string.

3. Place quail on an aluminum foil-lined jelly-roll pan or in a shallow roasting pan, and sprinkle with salt.

4. Bake at 450° for 10 minutes. Brush quail generously with room-temperature fig mixture. Reduce oven temperature to 400°. Bake quail 30 more minutes or until leg meat is no longer pink, basting with fig mixture every 10 minutes.

5. Place reserved chilled fig mixture in a small saucepan; stir in dry red wine, and cook over low heat, stirring often, 2 minutes or until thoroughly heated. Serve quail with sauce.

Make Ahead: Prepare recipe as directed through Step 3. Cover and chill up to 8 hours. Let stand at room temperature 15 minutes before proceeding with Steps 4 and 5.

Try this twist!

Fig-and-Balsamic-Glazed Cornish Hens: Substitute 4 (1¼- to 1½-lb.) cornish hens for quail. Prepare Step 1 as directed; omit Step 2. Rinse hens with cold water, and pat dry. Place hens, breast sides down, on a cutting board. Cut hens through backbone using kitchen shears to make 2 halves. Proceed with recipe as directed in Steps 3 through 5, increasing second bake time (at 400°) to 45 minutes. Let stand 10 minutes before serving.

GRILLED TURKEY BREAST

MAKES: 8 servings ▪ HANDS-ON TIME: 20 min. ▪ TOTAL TIME: 9 hours, 35 min., including salsa

$\frac{1}{3}$ cup kosher salt
$\frac{1}{3}$ cup sugar
3   bay leaves
2   jalapeño peppers, halved
2   Tbsp. cumin seeds
1   (5- to 6-lb.) boned, skin-on fresh
    turkey breast*
Vegetable cooking spray
1   Tbsp. table salt
1   Tbsp. cumin seeds
1   Tbsp. paprika
2   tsp. freshly ground black pepper
1   tsp. ground coriander
1   tsp. dried oregano
Parsley-Mint Salsa Verde

1. Stir together kosher salt, next 4 ingredients, and 2 qt. water in a large, deep food-safe container or stockpot until sugar dissolves. Add turkey. Chill 8 hours or overnight, turning once.

2. Coat cold cooking grate of grill with cooking spray, and place on grill. Light 1 side of grill, heating to 350° to 400° (medium-high) heat; leave other side unlit. Remove turkey from brine. Rinse turkey, drain well, and pat dry with paper towels.

3. Stir together table salt and next 5 ingredients. Rub skin of turkey with mixture.

4. Place turkey, skin side down, over lit side of grill, and grill, without grill lid, 4 to 5 minutes or until slightly charred. Transfer to unlit side, skin side up. Grill, covered with grill lid, 30 to 40 more minutes or until a meat thermometer inserted into thickest portion registers 165°. Return turkey, skin side down, to lit side, and grill, covered with grill lid, 4 to 5 more minutes or until skin is crisp.

5. Remove turkey from heat; cover loosely with aluminum foil. Let stand 10 minutes. Serve with salsa verde.

Frozen turkey breast, thawed, may be substituted.

Parsley-Mint Salsa Verde

MAKES: 1¾ cups ▪ HANDS-ON TIME: 15 min. ▪ TOTAL TIME: 35 min.

$\frac{2}{3}$ cup extra virgin olive oil
$\frac{1}{3}$ cup sherry vinegar
$\frac{1}{4}$ cup finely chopped shallots
2   garlic cloves, finely chopped
1   tsp. table salt
$\frac{1}{2}$ tsp. freshly ground black pepper
1   cup chopped fresh flat-leaf
    parsley
$\frac{3}{4}$ cup chopped fresh mint

Whisk together first 6 ingredients and 2 Tbsp. water until salt dissolves. Whisk in parsley and mint. Let stand 20 minutes.

TURKEY TENDERLOINS
with Madeira Gravy

MAKES: 12 servings ▪ **HANDS-ON TIME:** 40 min. ▪ **TOTAL TIME:** 3 hours, 10 min.

3   cups dry Madeira or fino sherry
¾   cup red wine vinegar
12   garlic cloves, crushed
18   fresh thyme sprigs
3   tsp. kosher salt, divided
4   lb. turkey tenderloins
2   Tbsp. vegetable oil, divided
1   tsp. freshly ground black pepper
3   Tbsp. butter
3   large shallots, finely chopped
2   tsp. sifted all-purpose flour
Garnish: fresh thyme sprigs

1. Stir together first 4 ingredients and 2 tsp. salt in a 2-qt. measuring cup until salt dissolves. Reserve 1¼ cups. Pour remaining mixture into a zip-top plastic freezer bag. Add tenderloins; press out air, seal, and chill 2 to 4 hours, turning every 30 minutes.

2. Preheat oven to 450°. Remove tenderloins from marinade, discarding marinade. Pat tenderloins dry. Brush with 1 Tbsp. oil, and sprinkle with pepper and remaining 1 tsp. salt.

3. Cook tenderloins, in batches, in remaining 1 Tbsp. hot oil in a large cast-iron skillet over high heat 2 to 3 minutes on each side or until browned. Transfer to a plate; discard oil. Reduce heat to medium. Add butter and shallots to skillet, and cook, stirring constantly, until butter melts. Stir in flour. Cook, stirring often, 3 minutes or until shallots are tender. Whisk in reserved 1¼ cups sherry mixture, and bring to a simmer. Simmer 2 to 3 minutes or until slightly thickened. Remove from heat, and add salt and pepper to taste. Place tenderloins in a 13- x 9-inch baking dish; pour sauce over tenderloins.

4. Bake at 450° for 10 to 12 minutes or until a meat thermometer inserted into thickest portion registers 165°. Transfer tenderloins to a cutting board, reserving gravy in baking dish. Cover loosely with aluminum foil, and let stand 10 minutes. Cut into ½-inch-thick medallions, and serve with gravy.

Make Ahead: *The turkey tenderloins marinate for 2 to 4 hours, making it an easy make-ahead dish. Prepare your side dishes while the tenderloins chill.*

HERB-ROASTED TURKEY

MAKES: 8 servings ▪ **HANDS-ON TIME:** 1 hour ▪ **TOTAL TIME:** 6 hours

1   (14-lb.) whole fresh turkey*
Kitchen string
1   tsp. dried thyme
1   tsp. ground sage
½   tsp. dried tarragon
3   tsp. table salt
1   tsp. freshly ground black pepper
¼   cup butter, softened
2   medium onions, chopped
2   carrots, chopped
2   celery ribs, chopped
1   garlic bulb, halved
1   cup dry white wine
Garnish: fresh sage leaves

1. Remove giblets and neck from turkey, and rinse turkey with cold water. Drain cavity well; pat dry. Tie ends of legs together with string; tuck wing tips under. Place, breast side up, on a lightly greased roasting rack in a large roasting pan. Let stand at room temperature 1 hour.

2. Preheat oven to 400°. Stir together thyme, next 2 ingredients, 1½ tsp. salt, and ½ tsp. black pepper; rub mixture into cavity of turkey. Rub butter over turkey. Sprinkle remaining salt and black pepper over outside of turkey; rub into skin. Arrange onions and next 3 ingredients around base of turkey in roasting pan; add wine and 1 cup water to pan.

3. Place turkey in oven; reduce oven temperature to 325°. Bake at 325° for 3 hours or until a meat thermometer inserted into thickest portion of thigh registers 160°.

4. Remove turkey from oven; increase heat to 425°. Baste turkey with pan juices, and let stand 15 minutes; return to oven. Bake at 425° for 10 to 15 minutes or until golden brown and thermometer registers 165°.

5. Let turkey stand in pan 30 minutes; transfer to a serving platter. Reserve pan drippings for Easy Turkey Gravy, if desired.

*Frozen whole turkey, thawed, may be substituted.

Easy Turkey Gravy

MAKES: 6 cups ▪ **HANDS-ON TIME:** 25 min. ▪ **TOTAL TIME:** 25 min.

Reserved pan drippings from
    Herb-Roasted Turkey
Chicken broth (up to 2½ cups),
    divided
¼   cup butter
¼   cup all-purpose flour

1. Pour reserved pan drippings through a wire-mesh strainer into a large measuring cup, discarding solids. Add broth to equal 3 cups.

2. Melt butter in a saucepan over medium heat; whisk in flour, and cook, whisking constantly, 10 to 12 minutes or until smooth and light brown. (Mixture should be color of peanut butter.) Gradually whisk in drippings mixture. Bring to a boil, whisking constantly. Reduce heat to medium-low; simmer, stirring occasionally, 5 minutes or until thickened. Add up to ½ cup broth for desired consistency. Add salt and pepper to taste.

APPLE-BOURBON TURKEY AND GRAVY

Apple slices and aromatic vegetables line the roasting pan, creating a colorful rack that adds terrific flavor to both the turkey and pan juices.

MAKES: 8 servings ▪ **HANDS-ON TIME:** 55 min. ▪ **TOTAL TIME:** 16 hours, 40 min.

4   cups apple juice
1   cup bourbon
½   cup firmly packed light brown
        sugar
1   (12- to 15-lb.) whole fresh turkey*
Cheesecloth
Kitchen string
4   celery ribs
4   large carrots
3   small apples, quartered
        or halved
1   large onion, sliced
¼   cup butter
¼   cup all-purpose flour
½   cup chicken broth (optional)

1. Stir together apple juice and next 2 ingredients, stirring until sugar dissolves.

2. Remove giblets and neck from turkey, and rinse turkey with cold water. Drain cavity well; pat dry. Place turkey in a large roasting pan. Dip cheesecloth in apple juice mixture; wring dry. Cover turkey with cheesecloth; pour apple juice mixture over cheesecloth, coating completely. Cover and chill 12 to 24 hours, basting occasionally with marinade.

3. Preheat oven to 325°. Remove turkey from pan, discarding cheesecloth and reserving 3 cups marinade. Sprinkle cavity with salt; rub into cavity. Add salt and freshly ground pepper on skin; rub into skin. Tie ends of legs together with string; tuck wing tips under.

4. Arrange celery and next 3 ingredients in a single layer in bottom of roasting pan. Place turkey, breast side up, on celery mixture; pour reserved marinade over turkey in pan.

5. Bake at 325° for 3 hours and 15 minutes to 4 hours or until a meat thermometer inserted into thickest portion of thigh registers 165°, basting every 30 minutes with pan juices and shielding with aluminum foil after 2 hours and 30 minutes to prevent excessive browning, if necessary. Remove from oven, and let stand 30 minutes.

6. Transfer turkey to a serving platter, reserving 2½ cups pan drippings. Pour reserved drippings through a fine wire-mesh strainer into a large measuring cup; discard solids.

7. Melt butter in a saucepan over medium heat; whisk in flour, and cook, whisking constantly, 1 to 2 minutes or until smooth. Gradually add drippings to pan, and bring to a boil. Reduce heat to medium, and simmer, stirring occasionally, 5 minutes or until gravy thickens. Add up to ½ cup chicken broth for desired consistency. Add salt and freshly ground black pepper to taste. Serve turkey with warm gravy.

*Frozen whole turkey, thawed, may be substituted.

PEACH-MUSTARD-GLAZED PORK TENDERLOIN

MAKES: 8 servings ▪ **HANDS-ON TIME:** 25 min. ▪ **TOTAL TIME:** 1 hour

2   (1¼-lb.) pork tenderloins
½   tsp. table salt
½   tsp. freshly ground black pepper
2   Tbsp. olive oil
2   Tbsp. butter
1   large shallot, minced
½   cup peach preserves
⅓   cup bourbon
¼   tsp. dried crushed red pepper
2   Tbsp. country-style Dijon
     mustard
½   cup reduced-sodium, fat-free
     chicken broth

1. Preheat oven to 400°. Sprinkle tenderloins with salt and black pepper. Cook in hot oil in a large ovenproof skillet over high heat 3 to 4 minutes on each side or until lightly browned.

2. Melt butter in a small skillet over medium-high heat; add shallot, and sauté 2 to 3 minutes or until tender. Remove from heat, and stir in peach preserves and next 3 ingredients. Cook over medium heat, stirring often, 1 minute or until preserves are melted. Pour mixture over tenderloins.

3. Bake at 400° for 20 minutes or until a meat thermometer inserted in thickest portion registers 150°. Transfer pork tenderloins to a cutting board, reserving pan drippings in skillet. Cover loosely with aluminum foil, and let stand 10 minutes before slicing.

4. Meanwhile, stir broth into reserved drippings, and cook over medium-high heat, stirring constantly, 5 minutes or until drippings are reduced by half. Serve with sliced tenderloins.

HOLIDAY TRADITION

Add a Southern touch to your Christmas dinner with this tangy glaze for pork tenderloin. Serve classic Southern side dishes such as green beans, grits, and squash casserole.

PORK ROAST
with Sweet Onion-Pumpkin Seed Relish

Be sure to ask your butcher to cut out the chine bone and french the rib rack for easy carving and an elegant presentation.

MAKES: 8 servings ▪ **HANDS-ON TIME:** 20 min. ▪ **TOTAL TIME:** 1 hour, 50 min.

1¼ tsp. table salt, divided
½ tsp. freshly ground black pepper
1 (5-lb.) 8-rib bone-in pork loin roast, chine bone removed
1 Tbsp. minced fresh rosemary
4 tsp. minced fresh thyme, divided
3 large sweet onions (about 2 lb.), cut into ½-inch-thick rings
2 Tbsp. olive oil
⅛ tsp. freshly ground black pepper
1 tsp. white wine vinegar
1 tsp. light brown sugar
¼ cup toasted pumpkin seeds

1. Preheat oven to 450°. Sprinkle 1 tsp. salt and ½ tsp. black pepper over pork; rub rosemary and 1 Tbsp. thyme over pork. Place pork in a lightly greased roasting pan.

2. Toss together onions, olive oil, ⅛ tsp. black pepper, and remaining ¼ tsp. salt until coated. Arrange onions around pork in pan.

3. Bake at 450° for 30 minutes; reduce oven temperature to 375°. Bake 50 more minutes or until a meat thermometer inserted into thickest portion registers 145°, stirring onions once. Transfer pork to a cutting board; cover loosely with aluminum foil, and let stand 10 minutes before slicing.

4. Meanwhile, coarsely chop onions; transfer to a medium bowl. Stir in vinegar, brown sugar, and remaining 1 tsp. thyme. Stir in toasted pumpkin seeds before serving. Serve pork with relish.

SPICY FRUIT-STUFFED PORK LOIN

with Roasted Pears and Onions

*Adding dried crushed red pepper to the stuffing keeps
this fruity dish savory and creates a fun flavor surprise.*

MAKES: 8 to 10 servings ▪ **HANDS-ON TIME:** 1 hour ▪ **TOTAL TIME:** 2 hours, 20 min.

PORK LOIN

2 (7-oz.) packages mixed dried
    fruit bits
2 Tbsp. dark brown sugar
1 Tbsp. chopped fresh sage
¼ tsp. dried crushed red pepper
1 (4-lb.) boneless pork loin
1½ tsp. kosher salt, divided
1½ tsp. coarsely ground black
    pepper, divided
Kitchen string
2 Tbsp. olive oil

ROASTED PEARS AND ONIONS

6 firm, ripe Seckel pears*
2 Tbsp. butter, melted
2 tsp. fresh lemon juice
2 tsp. honey**
¼ tsp. finely chopped fresh
    rosemary
¼ tsp. kosher salt
¼ tsp. freshly ground black pepper
2 (10-oz.) packages cipollini
    onions, peeled

GLAZE

½ cup pear preserves

1. Prepare Pork Loin: Bring first 4 ingredients and 1 cup water
to a boil in a small saucepan over medium-high heat. Cook
2 minutes, stirring once. Remove from heat, and cool completely
(about 40 minutes).
2. Meanwhile, butterfly pork by making a lengthwise cut down
center of 1 flat side, cutting to within ½ inch of other side. (Do
not cut all the way through pork.) Open pork, forming a
rectangle, and place between 2 sheets of heavy-duty plastic
wrap. Flatten to ½-inch thickness using a meat mallet or rolling
pin. Sprinkle with ½ tsp. each salt and black pepper.
3. Spoon fruit mixture over pork, leaving a ½-inch border
around edges. Roll up pork, jelly-roll fashion, starting at 1 long
side. Tie with string at 1½-inch intervals. Sprinkle with remaining
1 tsp. salt and 1 tsp. pepper.
4. Preheat oven to 375°. Brown pork in hot oil in a large
roasting pan over medium-high heat until browned on all sides
(about 2 to 3 minutes per side). Place pork seam side down.
5. Prepare Roasted Pears and Onions: Cut pears in half
lengthwise, and remove core. Stir together butter and next
5 ingredients. Stir in onions; gently stir in pear halves. Spoon
mixture around roast in roasting pan.
6. Bake at 375° for 1 hour to 1 hour and 5 minutes or until a
meat thermometer inserted into thickest portion of stuffing
registers 135°, stirring pear mixture halfway through. Cover with
aluminum foil, and let stand 15 minutes.
7. Prepare Glaze: Microwave preserves in a microwave-safe
bowl at HIGH 1 minute or until thoroughly heated. Pour warm
preserves over pork. Slice pork, and serve with Roasted Pears
and Onions and pan juices.

*3 firm, ripe Bartlett pears may be substituted. Core pears, and cut into
4 wedges each.
**Sugar may be substituted.*

HONEY-BOURBON-GLAZED HAM

MAKES: 15 servings ▪ **HANDS-ON TIME:** 20 min. ▪ **TOTAL TIME:** 3 hours, 20 min.

1 (9$\frac{1}{4}$-lb.) fully cooked,
   bone-in ham
40 whole cloves
$\frac{1}{2}$ cup firmly packed light brown
   sugar
$\frac{1}{2}$ cup bourbon
$\frac{1}{2}$ cup honey
$\frac{1}{3}$ cup Creole mustard
$\frac{1}{3}$ cup molasses
Garnish: fresh fruit

1. Preheat oven to 350°. Remove skin from ham, and trim fat to ¼-inch thickness. Make shallow cuts in fat 1 inch apart in a diamond pattern; insert cloves in centers of diamonds. Place ham in an aluminum foil-lined 13- x 9-inch pan.

2. Stir together brown sugar and next 4 ingredients; spoon over ham.

3. Bake at 350° on lower oven rack 2 hours and 30 minutes, basting with pan juices every 30 minutes. Shield ham with aluminum foil after 1 hour to prevent excessive browning, if necessary. Remove from oven, and let stand 30 minutes before serving.

Try this twist!

Honey-Bourbon Boneless Glazed Ham: Substitute 1 (4-lb.) smoked, fully cooked boneless ham for bone-in ham. Reduce cloves to 3 (do not insert into ham). Stir together brown sugar mixture as directed in Step 2; stir in cloves. Place ham in an aluminum foil-lined 13- x 9-inch pan. Pour sauce over ham. Bake as directed, reducing bake time to 1 hour, and basting after 30 minutes.

HONEY-CURRY-GLAZED LAMB

Consider ordering the lamb roasts from your butcher a few days ahead.

MAKES: 6 servings ▪ **HANDS-ON TIME:** 15 min. ▪ **TOTAL TIME:** 1 hour, 30 min., including Roasted Grapes and Cranberries

2 (8-rib) lamb rib roasts
    (2½ lb. each), trimmed
1 Tbsp. red curry powder
1½ tsp. kosher salt
1½ tsp. freshly ground black pepper
5 Tbsp. olive oil
2 Tbsp. honey
Garnish: fresh rosemary
Roasted Grapes and Cranberries

1. Preheat oven to 425°. Sprinkle lamb on all sides with curry powder, salt, and black pepper. Let stand 30 minutes.

2. Cook lamb in 1 Tbsp. hot oil in a 12-inch cast-iron skillet over medium heat 6 to 7 minutes, turning often to brown tops and sides. Place lamb, meat side up, in skillet. Stir together honey and remaining 4 Tbsp. olive oil; brush mixture on tops and sides of lamb.

3. Bake at 425° for 15 to 18 minutes or until a meat thermometer inserted into thickest portion registers 130°. Remove lamb from oven; let stand 10 minutes. Cut into chops, and serve with Roasted Grapes and Cranberries.

Roasted Grapes and Cranberries

This accompaniment pairs well with both lamb and pork dishes.
You can also add it to a cheese tray for a unique touch.

MAKES: 6 servings ▪ **HANDS-ON TIME:** 5 min. ▪ **TOTAL TIME:** 20 min.

6 to 8 seedless red grape clusters
    (about 1 lb.)
1 cup fresh cranberries
1 Tbsp. olive oil
1 tsp. chopped fresh rosemary

1. Preheat oven to 400°. Place grape clusters on a 15- x 10-inch jelly-roll pan. Stir together cranberries and next 2 ingredients. Spoon mixture over grape clusters.

2. Bake at 400° for 15 to 18 minutes or until grapes begin to blister and cranberries start to pop, shaking pan occasionally. Serve immediately, or let stand up to 4 hours.

RED WINE-BRAISED BRISKET
with Caramelized Onions

MAKES: 8 servings ▪ **HANDS-ON TIME:** 1 hour, 15 min. ▪ **TOTAL TIME:** 5 hours, 45 min.

1   *(4-lb.) beef brisket flat, cut into 3 pieces*

1½ *tsp. table salt*

1½ *tsp. black pepper*

2   *Tbsp. vegetable oil*

3   *large white onions, cut in half and thinly sliced (6 loosely packed cups, about 3 lb.)*

4   *shallots, sliced*

1   *tsp. sugar*

1   *(750-milliliter) bottle dry red wine*

1½ *tsp. chopped fresh rosemary, divided*

1   *(10-oz.) package cipollini onions, peeled*

1. Preheat oven to 350°. Sprinkle all sides of brisket pieces with salt and black pepper. Cook brisket, in batches, in hot oil in an ovenproof Dutch oven over medium-high heat until browned on all sides (about 15 minutes). Transfer to a plate, reserving drippings in Dutch oven.

2. Add white onions and shallots to hot drippings in Dutch oven, and sprinkle with sugar. Cook over medium heat, stirring often, 25 minutes or until onions are soft and caramelized. Stir in wine and 1 tsp. rosemary; add brisket. Top with cipollini onions; cover.

3. Bake at 350° for 4 hours or until brisket is tender. Remove from oven. Cover and let stand at room temperature 30 minutes. Transfer brisket to a cutting board and onions to a large bowl, reserving liquid in Dutch oven. Cover brisket and onions loosely with aluminum foil.

4. Bring reserved liquid to a boil over high heat, stirring often, 10 minutes or until liquid is reduced by half. Stir in onions and remaining ½ tsp. rosemary. Cut brisket across the grain into thick slices. Serve with onion mixture.

Note: *We tested with Rex-Goliath Merlot.*

While the brisket braises into melting tenderness in a bath of red wine and onions, you'll have time to make side dishes.

HERB-AND-POTATO CHIP-CRUSTED BEEF TENDERLOIN

Let your guests in on the secret to this beef tenderloin's crispy herb coating and rich, salty seasoning: potato chips!

MAKES: 6 to 8 servings ▪ **HANDS-ON TIME:** 40 min. ▪ **TOTAL TIME:** 2 hours, 20 min.

1   (4- to 5-lb.) beef tenderloin, trimmed
3   tsp. kosher salt, divided
¾   cup panko (Japanese breadcrumbs)
3   garlic cloves, pressed
2   tsp. coarsely ground black pepper, divided
3   Tbsp. olive oil, divided
1¼ cups crushed, plain kettle-cooked potato chips
¼   cup finely chopped fresh parsley
1   Tbsp. finely chopped fresh thyme
1   bay leaf, crushed
1   egg white, lightly beaten
1   Tbsp. Dijon mustard
Garnish: sage leaves

1. Preheat oven to 400°. Sprinkle tenderloin with 2 tsp. salt. Let stand 30 to 45 minutes.

2. Meanwhile, sauté panko, garlic, 1 tsp. black pepper, and remaining 1 tsp. salt in 1 Tbsp. hot oil in a skillet over medium heat 2 to 3 minutes or until deep golden brown. Let cool completely (about 10 minutes). Stir in potato chips and next 4 ingredients.

3. Pat tenderloin dry with paper towels, and sprinkle with remaining 1 tsp. black pepper. Brown beef in remaining 2 Tbsp. hot oil in a roasting pan over medium-high heat until browned on all sides (about 2 to 3 minutes per side). Transfer tenderloin to a wire rack in an aluminum foil-lined jelly-roll pan. Let stand 10 minutes.

4. Spread mustard over tenderloin. Press panko mixture onto top and sides of tenderloin.

5. Bake at 400° for 40 to 45 minutes or until coating is crisp and a meat thermometer inserted into thickest portion of tenderloin registers 130° (rare). Let stand 10 minutes.

Note: *We tested with Lay's Kettle Cooked Original Potato Chips. For medium-rare, cook tenderloin to 135°; for medium, cook to 150°.*

DECADENT DESSERTS

From cakes to cookies, satisfy everyone's sweet tooth with these scrumptious recipes. They make a delicious ending to any meal or are just perfect for a holiday gift.

PEAR DUMPLINGS

MAKES: 6 servings ▪ **HANDS-ON TIME:** 40 min. ▪ **TOTAL TIME:** 1 hour, 20 min.

3 cups all-purpose flour
2 tsp. baking powder
1 tsp. table salt
1 cup shortening
¾ cup milk
6 ripe Bosc pears
¼ cup firmly packed light
    brown sugar
1½ cups chopped macadamia nuts
1 tsp. ground cinnamon
¼ cup butter, softened
1½ cups granulated sugar
Orange peel strips of 1 medium
    orange
1 (3-inch) piece fresh ginger
1 Tbsp. butter
Garnishes: orange slices, cinnamon
    sticks, fresh mint

1. Preheat oven to 375°. Stir together first 3 ingredients; cut shortening into flour mixture with a pastry blender or fork until crumbly. Gradually add milk, stirring just until dry ingredients are moistened.

2. Turn dough out onto a lightly floured surface, and knead lightly 4 to 5 times. Shape into a 12-inch log. Cut log into 6 (2-inch) pieces. Shape each into a disk, and roll each into an 8-inch circle on a lightly floured surface.

3. Peel pears, reserving peels. Core each pear from bottom, leaving top 2 inches and stems intact.

4. Stir together brown sugar and next 2 ingredients; spoon about 1½ Tbsp. brown sugar mixture into each pear cavity, pressing firmly. Sprinkle remaining sugar mixture in center of pastry circles (about 1½ Tbsp. each). Place 1 pear in center of each pastry circle. Dot pears with ¼ cup softened butter. Press dough around pears with palms of hands, sealing around stem. Place in a lightly greased 13- x 9-inch baking dish.

5. Bake at 375° for 40 to 50 minutes, shielding with aluminum foil after 30 minutes to prevent excessive browning, if necessary.

6. Bring granulated sugar, next 3 ingredients, reserved pear peels, and 1½ cups water to a boil over medium-high heat, stirring constantly. Boil, stirring constantly, 1 minute or until sugar dissolves. Reduce heat to low. Cook, stirring occasionally, 5 minutes. Pour through a wire-mesh strainer into a bowl; discard solids. Pour syrup over dumplings. Serve immediately.

WRAP IT UP

Present friends and neighbors with a gift box filled
with fresh pears. Attach this recipe to the box
for the perfect presentation.

APPLE-CHERRY COBBLER WITH PINWHEEL BISCUITS

MAKES: 8 to 10 servings ■ **HANDS-ON TIME:** 1 hour ■ **TOTAL TIME:** 1 hour, 15 min.

APPLE-CHERRY FILLING

8   large Braeburn apples, peeled and cut into ½-inch-thick wedges (about 4 ½ lb.)
2   cups granulated sugar
¼   cup all-purpose flour
¼   cup butter
1   (12-oz.) package frozen cherries, thawed and well drained
1   tsp. lemon zest
⅓   cup fresh lemon juice
1   tsp. ground cinnamon

PINWHEEL BISCUITS

2¼   cups all-purpose flour
¼   cup granulated sugar
2¼   tsp. baking powder
¾   tsp. salt
¾   cup cold butter, cut into pieces
⅔   cup milk
⅔   cup firmly packed light brown sugar
2   Tbsp. butter, melted
¼   cup finely chopped roasted unsalted almonds

1. Prepare Filling: Preheat oven to 425°. Toss together first 3 ingredients. Melt ¼ cup butter in a large skillet over medium-high heat; add apple mixture. Cook, stirring often, 20 to 25 minutes or until apples are tender and syrup thickens. Remove from heat; stir in cherries and next 3 ingredients. Spoon apple mixture into a lightly greased 3-qt. baking dish. Bake at 425° for 12 minutes, placing a baking sheet on oven rack directly below baking dish to catch any drips.

2. Prepare Biscuits: Stir together 2 ¼ cups flour and next 3 ingredients in a large bowl. Cut butter into flour mixture with a pastry blender or fork until crumbly; stir in milk. Turn dough out onto a lightly floured surface; knead 4 to 5 times. Roll dough into a 12-inch square. Combine brown sugar and 2 Tbsp. melted butter; sprinkle over dough, patting gently. Sprinkle with almonds. Roll up, jelly-roll fashion; pinch seams and ends to seal. Cut roll into 12 (1-inch) slices. Place slices in a single layer on top of apple mixture.

3. Bake at 425° for 15 to 17 minutes or until biscuits are golden.

AMBROSIA CHESS TARTS

MAKES: 14 tarts ■ **HANDS-ON TIME:** 30 min. ■ **TOTAL TIME:** 2 hours, 20 min.

2   (14.1-oz.) packages refrigerated
       piecrusts*
1½ cups sugar
1   Tbsp. all-purpose flour
1   Tbsp. plain white cornmeal
½ tsp. table salt
4   large eggs
½ cup cream of coconut
⅓ cup butter, melted
¼ cup fresh lemon juice
1   cup sweetened flaked coconut
1   (8-oz.) can crushed pineapple
2   Tbsp. orange zest
Toppings: toasted coconut,
       sweetened whipped cream,
       orange sections, fresh
       rosemary sprigs

1. Preheat oven to 450°. Cut piecrusts into 14 (4½-inch) rounds. Press each dough round into a lightly greased 3½-inch brioche mold, pressing up sides. Fold dough over edge of molds, and pinch to secure. Arrange molds on a baking sheet. Bake 7 to 8 minutes or until lightly browned. Cool completely on baking sheet on a wire rack (about 30 minutes). Reduce oven temperature to 350°.

2. Meanwhile, whisk together sugar and next 3 ingredients in a large bowl; add eggs and next 3 ingredients, and whisk until blended. Stir in coconut and next 2 ingredients. Spoon coconut mixture into cooled pastry shells, filling almost full.

3. Bake at 350° for 22 to 25 minutes or until golden brown and centers of tarts are almost set. (Filling will continue to cook as it cools.) Cool tarts completely on baking sheet on wire rack (about 1 hour). Loosen tarts from molds using a small knife; remove tarts from molds. Serve with desired toppings.

*2 (8- or 10-oz.) packages frozen tart shells may be substituted. Bake as directed in Step 1.

HOLIDAY TRADITION

Adding ambrosia to the Christmas day dinner is a tradition among many families in the South. The biggest debate can be over whether or not to add marshmallows or pecans. These delicious Ambrosia Chess Tarts add a festive twist on this holiday classic.

BOURBON-CREAM CHEESE BROWNIES

MAKES: 16 brownies ▪ **HANDS-ON TIME:** 30 min. ▪ **TOTAL TIME:** 2 hours, 10 min.

4   (1-oz.) unsweetened chocolate
      baking squares
¾   cup butter
½   cup firmly packed light brown
      sugar
1¾ cups granulated sugar, divided
4   large eggs, divided
1   tsp. vanilla extract
⅛   tsp. table salt
1   cup all-purpose flour
1   (8-oz.) package cream cheese,
      softened
2   Tbsp. all-purpose flour
¼   cup bourbon

1. Preheat oven to 350°. Line bottom and sides of a 9-inch square pan with aluminum foil, allowing 2 to 3 inches to extend over sides; lightly grease foil.

2. Microwave chocolate squares and butter in a large microwave-safe bowl at HIGH 1½ to 2 minutes or until melted and smooth, stirring at 30-second intervals. Whisk in brown sugar and 1½ cups granulated sugar. Add 3 eggs, 1 at a time, whisking just until blended after each addition. Whisk in vanilla, salt, and 1 cup flour. Spread half of batter in prepared pan.

3. Beat cream cheese at medium speed with an electric mixer until smooth; add 2 Tbsp. flour and remaining ¼ cup granulated sugar, beating until blended. Add bourbon and remaining 1 egg, beating until blended.

4. Slowly pour cream cheese mixture over batter in pan; top with remaining batter, and swirl together gently with a knife.

5. Bake at 350° for 40 to 45 minutes or until a wooden pick inserted in center comes out with a few moist crumbs. Cool completely in pan on a wire rack (about 1 hour). Lift brownies from pan, using foil sides as handles. Gently remove foil; and cut brownies into 16 squares.

BOURBON BALLS

MAKES: about 5 dozen ▪ **HANDS-ON TIME:** 30 min. ▪ **TOTAL TIME:** 53 min.

1   (12-oz.) package vanilla wafers,
      finely crushed
1   cup toasted chopped pecans
¾   cup powdered sugar
2   Tbsp. unsweetened cocoa
½   cup bourbon
2½ Tbsp. light corn syrup
Powdered sugar

1. Stir together wafers and next 3 ingredients in a large bowl until well blended.

2. Stir together bourbon and corn syrup in a small bowl until well blended. Pour bourbon mixture over wafer mixture, stirring until blended. Shape into 1-inch balls; roll in powdered sugar. Cover and chill up to 2 weeks.

BOURBON-CREAM
CHEESE BROWNIES

DOUBLE CHOCOLATE
CHIP COOKIES
(PAGE 151)

BOURBON BALLS

peace
love AND joy

RED VELVET BROWNIES

RED VELVET BROWNIES

MAKES: about 2 dozen ▪ **HANDS-ON TIME:** 20 min. ▪ **TOTAL TIME:** 1 hour, 50 min.

1 (4-oz.) bittersweet chocolate baking bar, chopped
¾ cup butter
2¼ cups sugar, divided
4 large eggs
1 (1-oz.) bottle red liquid food coloring
¼ tsp. peppermint extract
2 tsp. vanilla extract, divided
1½ cups all-purpose flour
⅛ tsp. table salt
½ (8-oz.) package cream cheese, softened
2 egg whites
2 Tbsp. all-purpose flour

1. Preheat oven to 350°. Line bottom and sides of a 13- x 9-inch pan with aluminum foil, allowing 2 inches to extend over sides; lightly grease. Microwave chocolate and butter in a microwave-safe bowl at HIGH 1½ to 2 minutes or until melted and smooth, stirring at 30-second intervals. Whisk in 2 cups sugar. Add eggs, 1 at a time, whisking just until blended after each addition. Add food coloring, peppermint extract, and 1 tsp. vanilla. Gently stir in 1½ cups flour and ⅛ tsp. salt. Pour into pan.

2. Beat cream cheese and remaining ¼ cup sugar at medium speed with an electric mixer until fluffy. Add egg whites and remaining 1 tsp. vanilla; beat until blended. Stir in 2 Tbsp. flour until smooth. Drop by heaping tablespoonfuls over batter in pan; gently swirl with a knife. Bake at 350° for 30 to 32 minutes. Cool completely in pan on a wire rack (about 1 hour). Lift from pan, using foil sides as handles. Remove foil; cut into squares.

DOUBLE CHOCOLATE CHIP COOKIES

MAKES: 2½ dozen ▪ **HANDS-ON TIME:** 45 min. ▪ **TOTAL TIME:** 5 hours, 48 min., including ganache

¾ cup butter, softened
¾ cup granulated sugar
¾ cup firmly packed dark brown sugar
2 large eggs
1½ tsp. vanilla extract
2½ cups all-purpose flour
1 tsp. baking soda
¾ tsp. salt
1 (12-oz.) package semisweet chocolate morsels
Parchment paper
BOURBON GANACHE:
1 (12-oz.) package semisweet chocolate morsels
½ cup whipping cream
3 Tbsp. bourbon
3 Tbsp. butter, softened
½ tsp. vanilla extract

1. Preheat oven to 350°. Beat butter and sugars at medium speed with a heavy-duty electric stand mixer until creamy. Add eggs, 1 at a time, beating just until blended after each addition. Add vanilla, beating until blended.

2. Combine flour and next 2 ingredients; gradually add to butter mixture, beating at low speed just until blended. Stir in morsels just until combined. Drop dough by level spoonfuls onto parchment paper-lined baking sheets, using a small cookie scoop.

3. Bake at 350° for 12 minutes or until golden brown. Remove from baking sheets to wire racks, and cool completely (about 30 minutes).

4. Prepare Ganache: Microwave chocolate morsels and ½ cup whipping cream in a 2-qt. microwave-safe bowl at MEDIUM 2½ minutes or until chocolate begins to melt, stirring at 30-second intervals. Whisk in bourbon, butter, and vanilla extract. Cover and chill, stirring occasionally, 1 hour and 30 minutes or until thickened to a spreadable consistency.

5. Spread Bourbon Ganache on flat side of half of cookies (about 1 Tbsp. per cookie); top with remaining cookies. Cover and chill cookies 2 hours or until ganache is firm.

RED VELVET CUPCAKES

MAKES: 2 dozen ■ HANDS-ON TIME: 25 min. ■ TOTAL TIME: 2 hours, 18 min., including frosting

¾ cup butter, softened
1½ cups sugar
3 large eggs
1 (1-oz.) bottle red liquid food coloring
1 tsp. vanilla extract
2½ cups all-purpose flour
3 Tbsp. unsweetened cocoa
½ tsp. salt
1 cup buttermilk
1 Tbsp. white vinegar
1 tsp. baking soda
24 paper baking cups
White Chocolate-Amaretto Frosting
Parchment paper
White candy coating
Garnishes: white chocolate snowflakes, red candy sprinkles

1. Preheat oven to 350°. Beat butter at medium speed with an electric mixer until fluffy; gradually add sugar, beating well. Add eggs, 1 at a time, beating until blended after each addition. Stir in food coloring and vanilla, blending well.
2. Combine flour, cocoa, and salt. Stir together buttermilk, vinegar, and baking soda in a 4-cup liquid measuring cup. (Mixture will bubble.) Add flour mixture to butter mixture alternately with buttermilk mixture, beginning and ending with flour mixture. Beat at low speed until blended after each addition. Place paper baking cups in 2 (12-cup) muffin pans; spoon batter into cups, filling three-fourths full.
3. Bake at 350° for 18 to 20 minutes or until wooden pick inserted in centers comes out clean. Remove cupcakes from pans to wire racks, and cool completely (about 45 minutes).
4. Pipe White Chocolate-Amaretto Frosting onto cupcakes.
5. To make snowflake, place lightly greased snowflake-shaped cutters on parchment paper; fill each cutter to ¼ inch with melted white candy coating. Let stand until firm; gently press to remove.

White Chocolate-Amaretto Frosting

MAKES: 4 cups ■ HANDS-ON TIME: 20 min. ■ TOTAL TIME: 50 min.

2 (4-oz.) white chocolate baking bars
⅓ cup heavy cream
1 cup butter, softened
6 cups sifted powdered sugar
¼ cup almond liqueur

1. Break chocolate baking bars into pieces. Microwave chocolate pieces and cream in a microwave-safe container at MEDIUM (50% power) 1 minute or until melted and smooth, stirring at 30-second intervals. (Do not overheat.) Cool to room temperature (about 30 minutes).
2. Beat butter and 1 cup powdered sugar at low speed with an electric mixer until blended. Add remaining 5 cups powdered sugar alternately with almond liqueur, beating at low speed until blended after each addition. Add white chocolate mixture; beat at medium speed until spreading consistency.

RUM-GLAZED SWEET POTATO CAKES

MAKES: 3 dozen ▪ **HANDS-ON TIME:** 40 min. ▪ **TOTAL TIME:** 1 hour, 15 min.

¾ cup golden raisins

⅓ cup dark rum

4 large eggs, at room temperature

2 cups granulated sugar

1 cup vegetable oil

2 tsp. vanilla extract

2 cups pureed roasted sweet
  potatoes

3 cups all-purpose flour

1½ tsp. ground cinnamon

1 tsp. baking powder

1 tsp. baking soda

½ tsp. fine sea salt

½ tsp. ground nutmeg

¾ cup buttermilk

½ cup firmly packed dark brown
  sugar

¼ cup butter

3 Tbsp. whipping cream

½ cup finely chopped toasted
  pecans

1. Stir together first 2 ingredients. Let stand 30 minutes.

2. Meanwhile, beat eggs and granulated sugar at high speed with an electric mixer 2 to 4 minutes or until thick and pale. Add oil and vanilla, beating at low speed just until blended. Add sweet potato puree, beating just until blended and stopping to scrape down sides as needed.

3. Preheat oven to 350°. Sift together flour and next 5 ingredients; add to egg mixture alternately with buttermilk, beginning and ending with flour mixture. Beat at low speed just until blended after each addition. Drain raisins, reserving rum. Fold raisins into batter. Spoon batter into 3 lightly greased 12-cup Bundt brownie pans, filling each three-fourths full.

4. Bake at 350° for 14 to 16 minutes or until a wooden pick inserted in center comes out clean. Cool in pans on lightly greased wire racks 5 minutes. Remove from pans to wire racks.

5. Meanwhile, bring brown sugar and next 2 ingredients to a boil in a heavy saucepan over medium-high heat. Boil, stirring constantly, 3 minutes or until mixture begins to thicken to a syrup-like consistency. Remove from heat; stir in reserved rum.

6. Pierce tops of cakes multiple times using a wooden pick. Dip top halves of cakes in glaze, and hold 1 to 2 seconds (to allow glaze to soak into cakes). Place, glazed sides up, on lightly greased racks. Sprinkle each cake with pecans.

Tip: To puree roasted sweet potatoes, peel potatoes as soon as they are slightly cool. Press pulp through a wire-mesh strainer with the back of a spoon. You'll need to roast about 1½ lb. potatoes for 2 cups puree.

CRANBERRY-APPLE-PUMPKIN BUNDT

MAKES: 12 servings ▪ **HANDS-ON TIME:** 30 min. ▪ **TOTAL TIME:** 4 hours, 10 min., including toppings

1½ cups peeled and diced Granny
    Smith apples
2 Tbsp. butter, melted
½ cup finely chopped sweetened
    dried cranberries
½ cup firmly packed light brown
    sugar
3 Tbsp. all-purpose flour
¾ cup finely chopped toasted pecans
2 cups granulated sugar
1 cup butter, softened
4 large eggs
1 (15-oz.) can pumpkin
1 Tbsp. vanilla extract
3 cups all-purpose flour
2 tsp. baking powder
2 tsp. pumpkin pie spice
½ tsp. baking soda
Maple Glaze
Sugared Pecans and Pepitas

1. Preheat oven to 325°. Toss diced apples in 2 Tbsp. melted butter to coat in a medium bowl; add cranberries and next 3 ingredients, and toss until well blended.

2. Beat granulated sugar and 1 cup softened butter at medium speed with an electric mixer until light and fluffy. Add eggs, 1 at a time, beating just until blended after each addition. Add pumpkin and vanilla; beat just until blended.

3. Stir together 3 cups flour and next 3 ingredients. Gradually add flour mixture to butter mixture, beating at low speed just until blended after each addition. Spoon half of batter into a greased and floured 10-inch (12-cup) Bundt pan. Spoon apple mixture over batter, leaving a ½-inch border around outer edge. Spoon remaining batter over apple mixture.

4. Bake at 325° for 1 hour and 10 minutes to 1 hour and 20 minutes or until a long wooden pick inserted in center comes out clean. Cool in pan on a wire rack 15 minutes. Remove from pan to wire rack; cool completely (about 2 hours).

5. Spoon hot Maple Glaze onto cooled cake. Arrange pecans and pepitas on top of cake.

Sugared Pecans and Pepitas

MAKES: 1 ½ cups ▪ **HANDS-ON TIME:** 5 min. ▪ **TOTAL TIME:** 17 min.

1 cup pecan halves and pieces
½ cup roasted, salted shelled
    pepitas (pumpkin seeds)
2 Tbsp. butter, melted
2 Tbsp. sugar

Preheat oven to 350°. Stir together first 3 ingredients. Spread in a single layer in a 13- x 9-inch pan. Bake 12 to 15 minutes or until toasted and fragrant, stirring halfway through. Remove from oven; toss with sugar. Cool completely in pan on a wire rack (about 30 minutes).

Maple Glaze

MAKES: 1 cup ▪ **HANDS-ON TIME:** 10 min. ▪ **TOTAL TIME:** 10 min.

½ cup pure maple syrup
2 Tbsp. butter
1 Tbsp. milk
1 tsp. vanilla extract
1 cup powdered sugar

Bring first 3 ingredients to a boil in a small saucepan over medium-high heat, stirring constantly; boil, stirring constantly, 2 minutes. Remove from heat; whisk in vanilla extract. Gradually whisk in sugar until smooth; stir gently 3 to 5 minutes or until mixture begins to thicken and cool slightly. Use immediately.

BROWN SUGAR-BOURBON BUNDT

MAKES: 12 servings ▪ **HANDS-ON TIME:** 20 min. ▪ **TOTAL TIME:** 2 hours, 35 min.

1   cup butter, softened
½   cup shortening
1   (16-oz.) package light brown sugar
5   large eggs
1   (5-oz.) can evaporated milk
½   cup bourbon
3   cups all-purpose flour
½   tsp. baking powder
½   tsp. table salt
1   Tbsp. vanilla bean paste
2   Tbsp. powdered sugar
Garnishes: candied oranges, magnolia leaves

1. Preheat oven to 325°. Beat butter and shortening at medium speed with a heavy-duty electric stand mixer until creamy. Gradually add brown sugar, beating at medium speed until light and creamy. Add eggs, 1 at a time, beating just until blended after each addition.

2. Stir together evaporated milk and bourbon in a bowl. Stir together flour, baking powder, and salt in another bowl. Add flour mixture to butter mixture alternately with milk mixture, beginning and ending with flour mixture. Beat at low speed just until blended after each addition. Stir in vanilla bean paste. Pour batter into a greased and floured 10-inch (12-cup) Bundt pan.

3. Bake at 325° for 1 hour and 5 minutes to 1 hour and 10 minutes or until a long wooden pick inserted in center comes out clean. Cool in pan on a wire rack 10 to 15 minutes; remove from pan to wire rack. Cool completely (about 1 hour). Dust lightly with powdered sugar.

WRAP IT UP

Package a homemade cake in a decorative cake box or on a pretty platter to give to a friend or teacher this Christmas. Best of all, it can be made ahead and frozen for up to a month.

BLACK FOREST POUND CAKE

This decadent dessert is an easy, one-pan twist on the traditional layered cake.

MAKES: 10 servings ▪ **HANDS-ON TIME:** 30 min. ▪ **TOTAL TIME:** 3 hours, 15 min., including sauce

⅔ cup butter, softened
1⅓ cups granulated sugar
⅔ cup firmly packed dark brown sugar
4 large eggs
1¼ tsp. vanilla extract, divided
1½ cups cake flour
½ cup unsweetened cocoa
½ tsp. salt
¼ tsp. baking soda
¾ cup sour cream
3 (1-oz.) bittersweet chocolate baking squares, finely chopped
Cherry Sauce
1¼ cups heavy cream
1 Tbsp. granulated sugar
Shaved bittersweet chocolate

1. Preheat oven to 325°. Beat butter at medium speed with a heavy-duty electric stand mixer until creamy. Gradually add 1⅓ cups granulated sugar and ⅔ cup brown sugar, beating until light and fluffy (about 5 minutes). Add eggs, 1 at a time, beating just until blended after each addition. Beat in 1 tsp. vanilla.

2. Whisk together flour and next 3 ingredients. Add to butter mixture alternately with sour cream, beginning and ending with flour mixture. Beat at low speed just until blended after each addition. Stir in chopped chocolate.

3. Pour batter into a greased and floured 10-inch round cake pan (with sides that are 3 inches high).

4. Bake at 325° for 1 hour and 10 minutes to 1 hour and 20 minutes or until a wooden pick inserted in center comes out clean. Cool in pan on a wire rack 15 minutes. Remove from pan to wire rack; cool completely (about 1 hour).

5. Place cake on a serving plate or cake stand. Slowly pour Cherry Sauce over cake. Beat heavy cream, 1 Tbsp. granulated sugar, and remaining ¼ tsp. vanilla at medium-high speed until soft peaks form. Dollop whipped cream onto cake, and sprinkle with shaved chocolate.

Cherry Sauce

We used Kirsch, a fruit brandy made with sweet cherries, but the brandy in your liquor cabinet will work just fine. This sauce is also delicious over an ice-cream sundae. Try it on pancakes and waffles, too.

MAKES: 1½ cups ▪ **HANDS-ON TIME:** 20 min. ▪ **TOTAL TIME:** 1 hour, 20 min.

2 (12-oz.) packages frozen cherries
⅓ cup sugar
⅓ cup cold water
3 tsp. cornstarch
2 Tbsp. cherry liqueur or brandy
Pinch of salt

Stir together first 4 ingredients in a medium saucepan. Cook over medium-low heat, stirring often, 12 to 15 minutes or until thickened. Remove from heat, and stir in remaining ingredients. Cool completely (about 1 hour).

BANANAS FOSTER UPSIDE-DOWN CAKE

MAKES: 8 servings ▪ **HANDS-ON TIME:** 20 min. ▪ **TOTAL TIME:** 1 hour, 10 min.

½ cup butter, softened and divided

1 cup firmly packed light brown sugar

2 Tbsp. rum

2 ripe bananas

½ cup chopped toasted pecans

¾ cup granulated sugar

2 large eggs

¾ cup milk

½ cup sour cream

1 tsp. vanilla extract

2 cups all-purpose baking mix

¼ tsp. ground cinnamon

1. Preheat oven to 350°. Melt ¼ cup butter in a lightly greased 10-inch cast-iron skillet or 9-inch round cake pan (with sides that are at least 2 inches high) over low heat. Remove from heat; stir in brown sugar and rum.

2. Cut bananas diagonally into ¼-inch-thick slices; arrange in concentric circles over brown sugar mixture. Sprinkle pecans over bananas.

3. Beat granulated sugar and remaining ¼ cup butter at medium speed with an electric mixer until blended. Add eggs, 1 at a time, beating just until blended after each addition. Add milk and next 2 ingredients; beat just until blended. Beat in baking mix and cinnamon until blended. (Batter will be slightly lumpy.) Pour batter over mixture in skillet. Place skillet on a foil-lined jelly-roll pan.

4. Bake at 350° for 40 to 45 minutes or until a wooden pick inserted in center comes out clean. Cool in skillet on a wire rack 10 minutes. Run a knife around edge to loosen. Invert onto a serving plate, spooning any topping in skillet over cake.

One quick flip and this upside-down cake tumbles from the skillet perfectly golden and party-ready with the familiar flavors of Bananas Foster.

TIRAMISÙ LAYER CAKE

MAKES: 10 to 12 servings ▪ **HANDS-ON TIME:** 45 min. ▪ **TOTAL TIME:** 6 hours, 40 min., including syrup and frosting

TIRAMISÙ CAKE LAYERS

½ cup butter, softened
½ cup shortening
2 cups sugar
⅔ cup milk
3 cups all-purpose flour
1 Tbsp. baking powder
1 tsp. salt
1 Tbsp. vanilla bean paste*
1 tsp. almond extract
6 egg whites
Garnishes: raspberries,
    strawberries, red currants,
    fresh mint

COFFEE SYRUP

½ cup sugar
⅔ cup strong brewed coffee
¼ cup brandy

MASCARPONE FROSTING

2 (8-oz.) packages mascarpone
    cheese
3 cups heavy cream
1 Tbsp. vanilla extract
⅔ cup sugar

1. Prepare cake layers: Preheat oven to 350°. Beat butter and shortening at medium speed with an electric mixer until fluffy; gradually add sugar, beating well.
2. Stir together milk and ⅔ cup water. Combine flour and next 2 ingredients; add to butter mixture alternately with milk mixture, beginning and ending with flour mixture. Beat at low speed just until blended after each addition. Stir in vanilla bean paste and almond extract.
3. Beat egg whites at high speed until stiff peaks form, and fold into batter. Spoon batter into 3 greased and floured 8-inch round cake pans.
4. Bake at 350° for 25 to 30 minutes or until a wooden pick inserted in center comes out clean. Cool in pans on wire racks 10 minutes; remove from pans to wire racks, and cool completely (about 1 hour).
5. Prepare Coffee Syrup: Combine sugar and ⅓ cup water in a microwave-safe bowl. Microwave at HIGH 1½ minutes or until sugar dissolves, stirring at 30-second intervals. Stir in coffee and brandy. Cool 1 hour.
6. Prepare Mascarpone Frosting: Stir mascarpone cheese in a large bowl just until blended. Beat cream and vanilla at low speed with an electric mixer until foamy; increase speed to medium-high and gradually add sugar, beating until stiff peaks form. (Do not overbeat, or cream will be grainy.) Gently fold whipped cream mixture into mascarpone cheese. Use immediately.
7. Pierce cake layers with a wooden pick, making holes 1 inch apart. Brush or spoon Coffee Syrup over layers.
8. Place 1 cake layer, brushed side up, on a cake stand or serving plate. Spread top with 1⅓ cups Mascarpone Frosting. Top with second cake layer, brushed side up, and spread with 1⅓ cups Mascarpone Frosting. Top with remaining cake layer, brushed side up. Spread top and sides of cake with remaining Mascarpone Frosting. Chill 4 hours before serving.

*Vanilla extract may be substituted.

PEPPERMINT-HOT CHOCOLATE CAKE

MAKES: 10 to 12 servings ▪ **HANDS-ON TIME:** 40 min. ▪ **TOTAL TIME:** 2 hours, 25 min., including filling and frosting

PEPPERMINT-HOT CHOCOLATE CAKE LAYERS

- ½ cup boiling water
- 1 (4-oz.) milk chocolate baking bar, chopped
- 1 cup butter, softened
- 2 cups sugar
- 4 large eggs, separated
- 1 tsp. vanilla extract
- 2 cups all-purpose flour
- ¼ cup unsweetened cocoa
- 1 tsp. baking soda
- 1 tsp. table salt
- 1 cup buttermilk

Fudge Filling
Peppermint Cream Frosting
Garnishes: French vanilla cream-filled rolled wafer cookies dusted with powdered sugar, hard peppermint candies, fresh mint sprig

FUDGE FILLING

- 1 (14-oz.) can sweetened condensed milk
- 1 (12-oz.) package semisweet chocolate morsels
- ¼ tsp. peppermint extract

PEPPERMINT CREAM FROSTING

- 1 (7-oz.) jar marshmallow crème
- 1 (8-oz.) container frozen whipped topping, thawed
- ⅛ tsp. peppermint extract

1. Prepare cake layers: Preheat oven to 350°. Grease and flour 3 (8-inch) round cake pans.

2. Pour boiling water over chocolate in a small heatproof bowl. Stir until chocolate is melted and smooth. Cool to room temperature (about 30 minutes).

3. Beat butter at medium speed with a heavy-duty electric stand mixer until creamy; gradually add sugar, beating until light and fluffy. Add egg yolks, 1 at a time, beating until blended after each addition. Add melted chocolate and vanilla, beating until blended. Combine flour and next 3 ingredients; add to butter mixture alternately with buttermilk, beginning and ending with flour mixture. Beat at low speed just until blended after each addition.

4. Beat egg whites at medium speed until soft peaks form; gently fold into batter. Pour batter into prepared pans.

5. Bake at 350° for 20 to 30 minutes or until a wooden pick inserted in center comes out clean. Cool in pans on wire racks 10 minutes; remove from pans to wire racks, and cool completely (about 40 minutes).

6. Prepare Fudge Filling: Combine sweetened condensed milk and chocolate morsels in a saucepan, and cook over medium-low heat, stirring constantly, 4 to 6 minutes or until chocolate is melted and smooth. Remove from heat; stir in peppermint extract. Cool filling to room temperature (about 20 minutes).

7. Prepare Peppermint Cream Frosting: Beat marshmallow crème, whipped topping, and peppermint extract at high speed with an electric mixer 1 to 2 minutes or until glossy, stiff peaks form.

8. Spread Fudge Filling between cake layers. Spread Peppermint Cream frosting on top and sides of cake.

Note: We tested with Nielsen-Massey Pure Peppermint Extract.

WHITE CHOCOLATE RUSSE

MAKES: 12 servings ▪ **HANDS-ON TIME:** 30 min. ▪ **TOTAL TIME:** 4 hours, 30 min.

4   (3.4-oz.) packages fat-free
    white chocolate instant
    pudding mix
3½ cups whole milk
2   tsp. grated orange rind
1   Tbsp. orange liqueur or orange
    juice, divided
1   tsp. vanilla extract
1   cup whipping cream, whipped
24 ladyfingers (2 [3-oz.] packages)
Garnishes: raspberries, powdered
    sugar, fresh mint leaves, white
    chocolate curls

1. Prepare packages of pudding mix according to package directions, using 3½ cups whole milk instead of skim milk. Stir in orange rind, orange liqueur, and vanilla. Gently fold in whipped cream.

2. Line bottom and sides of a 9-inch springform pan with ladyfingers. Spoon pudding mixture into pan. Cover and chill at least 4 hours or until dessert is set.

3. Place dessert on a serving platter; carefully remove sides of pan.

Note: Here's an easy way to arrange ladyfingers in the springform pan: Simply remove rows of connected ladyfingers intact from their package, and unfold them into the bottom of pan, and then again around sides of pan.

WHITE CHOCOLATE-CRANBERRY CHEESECAKE

MAKES: 6 to 8 servings ■ **HANDS-ON TIME:** 35 min. ■ **TOTAL TIME:** 12 hours, 40 min., plus 1 day for chilling

CRANBERRY TOPPING

1   (12-oz.) package fresh
        cranberries
1   cup sugar
½   cup seedless raspberry jam
Garnish: fresh mint leaves

PIECRUST

1   (9-oz.) package chocolate
        wafer cookies
½   (4-oz.) semisweet chocolate
        baking bar, chopped
½   cup butter, melted
1⅓ cups sugar

CHEESECAKE FILLING

1   (6-oz.) package white chocolate
        baking squares, chopped
¼   cup whipping cream
2   (8-oz.) packages cream cheese,
        softened
2   Tbsp. all-purpose flour
⅓   cup sugar
4   large eggs
½   cup chopped sweetened
        dried cranberries
½   (4-oz.) semisweet chocolate
        baking bar, finely chopped
¼   cup amaretto liqueur

1. Prepare Topping: Bring first 2 ingredients and ¼ cup water to a boil in a 3-qt. saucepan over medium-high heat, stirring often. Boil, stirring often, 6 to 8 minutes or until mixture thickens to a syrup-like consistency. Remove from heat, and stir in jam. Cool completely (about 1 hour). Cover and chill 8 hours.

2. Prepare Piecrust: Preheat oven to 350°. Pulse wafer cookies and chopped semisweet chocolate in a food processor 8 to 10 times or until mixture resembles fine crumbs. Stir together crumb mixture, melted butter, and ⅓ cup sugar; firmly press on bottom, up sides, and onto lip of a lightly greased 10-inch pie plate. Bake 10 minutes. Transfer to a wire rack, and cool completely (about 30 minutes). Reduce oven temperature to 325°.

3. Prepare Cheesecake Filling: Microwave white chocolate and whipping cream at MEDIUM (50% power) 1 to 1½ minutes or until melted and smooth, stirring at 30-second intervals.

4. Beat cream cheese, flour, and ⅓ cup sugar at medium speed with an electric mixer 1 minute or until creamy and smooth. Add eggs, 1 at a time, beating just until blended after each addition. Add cranberries, next 2 ingredients, and white chocolate mixture. Beat at low speed just until blended. Spoon batter into prepared crust.

5. Bake at 325° for 30 to 35 minutes or until set. Cool completely on a wire rack (about 2 hours). Cover and chill 8 hours. Spoon topping over pie before serving.

PUMPKIN-PECAN CHEESECAKE

MAKES: 12 servings ▪ **HANDS-ON TIME:** 25 min. ▪ **TOTAL TIME:** 11 hours, 32 min., including Praline Topping and Pie-Glazed Pecans

2   cups graham cracker crumbs
⅓   cup finely chopped pecans
5   Tbsp. butter, melted
3   Tbsp. light brown sugar
4   (8-oz.) packages cream cheese, softened
1   cup granulated sugar
1   tsp. vanilla extract
4   large eggs
1½   cups canned pumpkin
1½   Tbsp. lemon juice
Praline Topping
Pie-Glazed Pecans
Garnish: fresh sage leaves

1. Preheat oven to 325°. Stir together first 4 ingredients in a bowl until well blended. Press mixture on bottom and 1½ inches up sides of a 9-inch springform pan. Bake 8 to 10 minutes or until lightly browned. Beat cream cheese and next 2 ingredients at medium speed with a heavy-duty electric stand mixer until blended and smooth. Add eggs, 1 at a time, beating just until blended after each addition. Add pumpkin and lemon juice, beating until blended. Pour batter into prepared crust. (Pan will be very full.)

2. Bake at 325° for 1 hour to 1 hour and 10 minutes or until almost set. Turn oven off. Let cheesecake stand in oven, with door closed, 15 minutes. Remove cheesecake from oven, and gently run a knife around outer edge of cheesecake to loosen from sides of pan. (Do not remove sides of pan.) Cool completely on a wire rack (about 1 hour). Cover and chill 8 to 24 hours. Remove sides and bottom of pan, and transfer cheesecake to a serving plate. Pour hot Praline Topping slowly over top of cheesecake, spreading to within ¼ inch of edge. Top with Pie-Glazed Pecans.

Praline Topping

MAKES: 1⅓ cups ▪ **HANDS-ON TIME:** 15 min. ▪ **TOTAL TIME:** 20 min.

1   cup firmly packed brown sugar
⅓   cup whipping cream
¼   cup butter
1   cup powdered sugar, sifted
1   tsp. vanilla extract

Bring first 3 ingredients to a boil in a 1-qt. saucepan over medium heat, stirring often. Boil, stirring occasionally, 1 minute; remove from heat. Gradually whisk in powdered sugar and vanilla until smooth. Let stand 5 minutes, whisking occasionally. Use immediately.

Pie-Glazed Pecans

MAKES: 2 cups ▪ **HANDS-ON TIME:** 15 min. ▪ **TOTAL TIME:** 35 min.

¼   cup dark corn syrup
2   Tbsp. sugar
2   cups pecan halves
Parchment paper
Vegetable cooking spray

Preheat oven to 350°. Stir together dark corn syrup and sugar. Add pecans; stir until pecans are coated. Line a jelly-roll pan with parchment paper; coat parchment paper with vegetable cooking spray. Spread pecans in a single layer in prepared pan. Bake at 350° for 15 minutes or until glaze bubbles slowly and thickens, stirring every 3 minutes. Transfer pan to a wire rack. Spread pecans in a single layer, separating individual pecans; cool completely. Cooled pecans should be crisp; if not, bake 5 more minutes.

CRANBERRY-APPLE PIE WITH PECAN SHORTBREAD CRUST

MAKES: 12 servings ▪ **HANDS-ON TIME:** 30 min. ▪ **TOTAL TIME:** 3 hours, 30 min.

CRUST

1½ cups butter, softened
¾ cup powdered sugar
3 cups all-purpose flour
1 cup finely chopped toasted
    pecans

FILLING

3 lb. Gala apples
1 cup firmly packed light
    brown sugar
¾ cup sweetened dried cranberries
¼ cup all-purpose flour
1 tsp. ground cinnamon
2 Tbsp. butter, melted

Garnishes: toasted pecan halves,
    powdered sugar

1. Prepare Crust: Preheat oven to 350°. Beat butter at medium speed with an electric mixer 1 minute or until creamy; add powdered sugar, beating well. Gradually add flour, beating at low speed until mixture is no longer crumbly and starts to come together into a ball. Stir in toasted pecans. Shape one-third of dough into an 8-inch log; wrap in plastic wrap, and chill until ready to use. Press remaining dough on bottom and up sides of a 9-inch springform pan. Cover and chill crust.

2. Prepare Filling: Peel apples; cut into ¼-inch-thick wedges. Toss together apples and next 4 ingredients. Spoon mixture into prepared crust. Drizzle with melted butter.

3. Cut reserved dough log into 8 (1-inch) pieces. Gently shape each piece into a 6- to 8-inch rope. Lightly press each rope to flatten into strips. Arrange strips in a lattice design over filling.

4. Bake at 350° for 1 hour to 1 hour and 10 minutes or until juices are thick and bubbly, crust is golden brown, and apples are tender when pierced with a long wooden pick, shielding with foil during last 30 minutes to prevent excessive browning. Cool completely in pan on a wire rack. Remove sides of pan.

CHOCOLATE-PECAN CHESS PIE

MAKES: 8 servings ▪ **HANDS-ON TIME:** 15 min. ▪ **TOTAL TIME:** 2 hours, 5 min.

½ (14.1-oz.) package refrigerated
   piecrusts
½ cup butter
2 (1-oz.) unsweetened chocolate
   baking squares
1 (5-oz.) can evaporated milk
   (⅔ cup)
2 large eggs
2 tsp. vanilla extract, divided
1½ cups granulated sugar
3 Tbsp. unsweetened cocoa
2 Tbsp. all-purpose flour
⅛ tsp. table salt
1½ cups pecan halves and pieces
⅔ cup firmly packed light brown
   sugar
1 Tbsp. light corn syrup

1. Preheat oven to 350°. Roll piecrust into a 13-inch circle on a lightly floured surface. Fit into a 9-inch pie plate; fold edges under, and crimp.
2. Microwave butter and chocolate squares in a large microwave-safe bowl at MEDIUM (50% power) 1½ minutes or until melted and smooth, stirring at 30-second intervals. Whisk in evaporated milk, eggs, and 1 tsp. vanilla.
3. Stir together granulated sugar and next 3 ingredients. Add sugar mixture to chocolate mixture, whisking until smooth. Pour mixture into prepared crust.
4. Bake pie at 350° for 40 minutes. Stir together pecans, next 2 ingredients, and remaining 1 tsp. vanilla; sprinkle over pie. Bake 10 more minutes or until set. Remove from oven to a wire rack, and cool completely (about 1 hour).

Dark, rich, and intensely chocolaty, this is our favorite new twist on pecan pie. Make it even more special and serve with sweetened whipped cream.

RED VELVET-RASPBERRY TIRAMISÙ TRIFLE

MAKES: 10 servings ▪ **HANDS-ON TIME:** 20 min. ▪ **TOTAL TIME:** 5 hours, 5 min., including madeleines

1   cup seedless raspberry jam
¼   cup black raspberry liqueur
¼   cup fresh orange juice
2   (8-oz.) containers mascarpone
     cheese
2   cups heavy cream
⅓   cup sugar
1   tsp. vanilla extract
Red Velvet Madeleines
3   (6-oz.) containers fresh
     raspberries

1. Whisk together first 3 ingredients in a small bowl.
2. Stir together mascarpone cheese in a large bowl, just until blended.
3. Beat heavy cream at high speed with an electric mixer until foamy; gradually add sugar and vanilla, beating until soft peaks form. Stir one-fourth of whipped cream into mascarpone using a rubber spatula; fold in remaining whipped cream.
4. Arrange one-third of Red Velvet Madeleines in a 3-qt. trifle dish; drizzle with one-third of jam mixture, top with 1 container of raspberries, and dollop raspberries with one-third of mascarpone mixture. Repeat layers twice. Cover and chill 4 to 24 hours before serving.

Red Velvet Madeleines

MAKES: 2 dozen ▪ **HANDS-ON TIME:** 15 min. ▪ **TOTAL TIME:** 45 min.

3   large eggs
2   egg yolks
¾   cup granulated sugar
1   tsp. vanilla extract
¾   cup butter, melted
2   Tbsp. red liquid food coloring
1⅓   cups cake flour
2   Tbsp. unsweetened cocoa
½   tsp. baking powder
¼   tsp. table salt

1. Preheat oven to 400°. Beat first 4 ingredients at medium-high speed with an electric mixer 5 minutes or until thick and pale. Add butter and food coloring, beating until blended.
2. Sift together cake flour and next 3 ingredients; fold into egg mixture. Spoon batter into 2 lightly greased shiny madeleine pans, filling three-fourths full (about 1 Tbsp. per madeleine).
3. Bake at 400° for 8 to 10 minutes or until centers of madeleines spring back when lightly touched. Immediately remove from pans to wire racks, and cool completely (about 20 minutes).

To make snowflake garnish, dust work surface with powdered sugar and roll out half of 1 (24-oz.) package white fondant to ¼ inch. Cut fondant with snowflake cutter. Transfer to baking sheets; let dry 12 hours.

BREAD & BUTTER

Serve these melt-in-your-mouth treats and their tasty accompaniments any time of day.

BASIL-BLACKBERRY
PRESERVES

ROSEMARY-PEAR
PRESERVES

MINT-PEPPER JELLY

BALSAMIC-STRAWBERRY
PRESERVES

MUSTARD-PEACH PRESERVES

MAKES: 1¾ cups ▪ **HANDS-ON TIME:** 15 min. ▪ **TOTAL TIME:** 1 hour, 15 min.

½ medium-size sweet onion, finely chopped

1 Tbsp. olive oil

1 cup peach preserves

¾ cup chopped dried peaches

¼ cup coarse-grained Dijon mustard

¼ tsp. table salt

¼ tsp. freshly ground black pepper

Sauté onion in hot oil in a large nonstick skillet, stirring often, over medium-high heat 5 to 6 minutes or until golden brown. Remove from heat, and stir in preserves and next 4 ingredients. Cover and chill 1 hour before serving. Refrigerate in an airtight container up to 1 week.

Flavorful Preserves

Serve any one of these fruit-and-herb mixtures with your favorite biscuit for a delicious classic combination.

Mint-Pepper Jelly: Stir together ½ cup pepper jelly and 1½ tsp. chopped fresh mint.

Basil-Blackberry Preserves: Stir together ½ cup blackberry preserves and 1½ to 2 tsp. chopped fresh basil.

Rosemary-Pear Preserves: Stir together ½ cup pear preserves and ½ tsp. chopped fresh rosemary.

Balsamic-Strawberry Preserves: Bring ¾ cup balsamic vinegar to a boil in a saucepan over medium-high heat. Reduce heat to medium low, and simmer, stirring occasionally, 18 to 20 minutes or until reduced to about 2 Tbsp. Let cool 10 minutes. Stir in 1 cup strawberry preserves.

VIDALIA ONION-AND-PEACH RELISH

You will need a canner, jar lifter, and canning rack. Look for a 9- or 12-piece canning kit, which will include all of these pieces and more.

MAKES: about 10 (8 oz.) jars ▪ **HANDS-ON TIME:** 1 hour, 10 min. ▪ **TOTAL TIME:** 1 hour, 40 min., plus 1 day for standing

10 (8 oz.) canning jars with metal
    lids and bands
2 cups sugar
2 cups apple cider vinegar
¼ cup gin
2 Tbsp. table salt
1 Tbsp. mustard seeds
1 tsp. celery salt
½ tsp. dried crushed red pepper
4 bay leaves, crushed
3 lb. Vidalia onions, finely chopped
3 lb. peaches, peeled and chopped
4 garlic cloves, thinly sliced

1. Bring canner half-full with water to a boil; reduce heat, and keep water simmering. Meanwhile, place 10 (8-oz.) jars in a large stockpot with water to cover; bring to a boil, reduce heat, and simmer. Place metal lids and bands in a large saucepan with water to cover; bring to a boil, and simmer. Remove hot jars 1 at a time using jar lifter.

2. Bring 2 cups water, 2 cups sugar, and next 7 ingredients to a boil in a Dutch oven over medium-high heat. Add onions, peaches, and garlic cloves; return to boil, and cook, stirring occasionally, 15 minutes.

3. Pour hot mixture into hot jars, filling to ½ inch from top. Remove air bubbles, and wipe jar rims. Cover immediately with metal lids, and screw on bands (snug but not too tight). Arrange filled jars in canning rack, and place in simmering water in canner; add additional boiling water as needed to cover by 1 to 2 inches. Bring water to a rolling boil; boil 10 minutes. Turn off heat, and let stand 5 minutes.

4. Remove jars from canner, and let stand at room temperature 24 hours. Test seals of jars by pressing center of each lid; if lids do not pop, jars are properly sealed. Store in a cool, dark place at room temperature up to 1 year.

WRAP IT UP

Prepare this relish in the summer when things aren't quite as busy. Package it in decorative glass jars tied with fabric and twine to give as gifts during the busy holiday season.

FLUFFY CREAM CHEESE BISCUITS

Three leavening ingredients—yeast, baking powder, and baking soda—ensure light biscuits every time.

MAKES: about 18 biscuits ▪ **HANDS-ON TIME:** 15 min. ▪ **TOTAL TIME:** 45 min.

1   (¼-oz.) envelope active dry yeast
¼   cup warm water (105° to 115°)
5   cups all-purpose flour
2   Tbsp. sugar
1   Tbsp. baking powder
1   tsp. baking soda
1   tsp. table salt
1   (8-oz.) package cold cream cheese, cut into pieces
½   cup cold butter, cut into pieces
1¼ cups buttermilk
Parchment paper
2   Tbsp. butter, melted

1. Preheat oven to 400°. Combine yeast and warm water in a small bowl; let stand 5 minutes.

2. Meanwhile, whisk together flour and next 4 ingredients in a large bowl; cut cream cheese and cold butter into flour mixture with a pastry blender or fork until crumbly.

3. Combine yeast mixture and buttermilk, and add to flour mixture, stirring just until dry ingredients are moistened. Turn dough out onto a lightly floured surface, and knead lightly 6 to 8 times (about 30 seconds to 1 minute), sprinkling with up to ¼ cup additional flour as needed to prevent sticking.

4. Roll dough to ¾-inch thickness. Cut with a 2½-inch round cutter, rerolling scraps once. Arrange biscuits on 2 parchment paper-lined baking sheets.

5. Bake at 400° for 13 to 15 minutes or until golden brown. Brush with melted butter.

BLUE CHEESE BUTTER

MAKES: 1 cup ▪ **HANDS-ON TIME:** 10 min. ▪ **TOTAL TIME:** 10 min.

1   (5-oz.) wedge soft ripened blue cheese, rind removed
½   cup butter
1   green onion, minced
2   Tbsp. chopped fresh parsley
1   tsp. Dijon mustard
¼   tsp. freshly ground black pepper

Let cheese and butter come to room temperature. Stir together cheese, butter, and remaining ingredients with a fork until thoroughly blended. Serve immediately. Refrigerate in an airtight container up to 1 week.

ICEBOX DINNER ROLLS

MAKES: 20 rolls ▪ **HANDS-ON TIME:** 30 min. ▪ **TOTAL TIME:** 9 hours, 35 min.

1   cup boiling water
6   Tbsp. shortening
½   cup sugar
1   tsp. table salt
1   (¼-oz.) envelope active dry yeast
¼   cup warm water (105° to 115°)
1   large egg, lightly beaten
4   cups all-purpose flour
¼   cup butter, melted and divided

1. Pour boiling water over shortening and next 2 ingredients in bowl of a heavy-duty electric stand mixer, and stir until shortening melts and sugar and salt completely dissolve. Let stand 10 minutes or until about 110°.

2. Meanwhile, combine yeast and warm water in a 1-cup liquid measuring cup; let stand 5 minutes.

3. Add yeast mixture and egg to shortening mixture, and beat at low speed until combined. Gradually add flour, beating at low speed 2 to 3 minutes or until flour is blended and dough is soft and smooth.

4. Place dough in a lightly greased bowl, turning to grease top. Cover and chill 8 to 24 hours.

5. Turn dough out onto a lightly floured surface, and knead until smooth and elastic (about 1 minute). Gently shape dough into 60 (1-inch) balls; place 3 dough balls in each cup of 2 lightly greased 12-cup muffin pans. (You will fill only 20 cups.) Brush rolls with half of melted butter.

6. Cover pans with plastic wrap, and let rise in a warm place (85°), free from drafts, 45 minutes to 1 hour or until doubled in bulk.

7. Preheat oven to 400°. Bake rolls for 8 to 12 minutes or until golden brown. Brush with remaining melted butter. Serve immediately.

HOLIDAY TRADITION

Complete your holiday dinner with a big batch of melt-in-your-mouth yeast rolls. Serve with monogrammed pats of butter made with a cookie cutter and a metal monogram stamp.

FRESH CORN SPOONBREAD

MAKES: 12 servings ■ **HANDS-ON TIME:** 30 min. ■ **TOTAL TIME:** 1 hour, 5 min.

1   cup self-rising white
        cornmeal mix
½   cup all-purpose flour
2   Tbsp. sugar
1   tsp. table salt
4   cups fresh corn kernels (about
        8 ears)
3   large eggs, lightly beaten
2   cups plain yogurt
¼   cup butter, melted
¼   cup chopped fresh chives
2   Tbsp. chopped fresh parsley
1   tsp. minced fresh thyme
Garnish: fresh thyme sprigs

1. Preheat oven to 350°. Stir together first 4 ingredients in a large bowl; make a well in center of mixture. Stir together corn and next 6 ingredients; add to cornmeal mixture, stirring just until dry ingredients are moistened. Divide mixture among 12 (6-oz.) lightly greased ramekins.
2. Bake at 350° for 35 to 40 minutes or until golden brown and set. Serve immediately.

Perfect individual servings of spoonbread serve as a more satisfying alternative to cornbread.

SWEET GREEN TOMATO CORN MUFFINS

If you're looking for a new twist for this year's crop of green tomatoes, try this Southern favorite.

MAKES: 2 dozen ▪ **HANDS-ON TIME:** 30 min. ▪ **TOTAL TIME:** 45 min.

2   *cups seeded, diced green tomatoes (about ¾ lb.)*
½   *cup sugar, divided*
½   *cup butter, melted and divided*
2   *cups self-rising white cornmeal mix*
2   *tsp. lemon zest*
5   *large eggs*
1   *(16-oz.) container sour cream*
Vegetable cooking spray
Fresh Basil Butter (optional)

1. Preheat oven to 450°. Sauté tomatoes and 2 Tbsp. sugar in 2 Tbsp. melted butter in a large skillet over medium-high heat 10 to 12 minutes or until tomatoes begin to caramelize and turn light brown.

2. Stir together cornmeal mix, lemon zest, and remaining 6 Tbsp. sugar in a large bowl; make a well in center of mixture. Whisk together eggs, sour cream, and remaining 6 Tbsp. butter; add to cornmeal mixture, stirring just until dry ingredients are moistened. Fold in tomatoes.

3. Generously coat small (¼-cup) brioche molds or muffin pans with cooking spray; spoon batter into molds, filling two-thirds full. Bake at 450° for 15 to 17 minutes or until a wooden pick inserted in center comes out clean. Serve with Fresh Basil Butter, if desired.

Fresh Basil Butter

MAKES: ½ cup ▪ **HANDS-ON TIME:** 5 min. ▪ **TOTAL TIME:** 5 min.

½   *cup butter, softened*
2   *Tbsp. finely chopped fresh basil*

Stir together butter and basil.

ANGEL BISCUITS

The addition of yeast will guarantee fluffy biscuits every time.

MAKES: about 2 dozen ▪ **HANDS-ON TIME:** 30 min. ▪ **TOTAL TIME:** 42 min.

1   (¼-oz.) envelope active dry yeast
¼   cup warm water (105° to 115°)
5   cups all-purpose flour
2   Tbsp. sugar
1   Tbsp. baking powder
1   tsp. baking soda
1   tsp. table salt
½   cup shortening, cut into pieces
½   cup cold butter, cut into pieces
1½ cups buttermilk

1. Preheat oven to 400°. Combine yeast and warm water in a 1-cup glass measuring cup; let stand 5 minutes.
2. Meanwhile, whisk together flour and next 4 ingredients in a large bowl; cut in shortening and butter with a pastry blender until crumbly.
3. Combine yeast mixture and buttermilk, and add to flour mixture, stirring just until dry ingredients are moistened. Turn dough out onto a lightly floured surface, and knead about 1 minute.
4. Roll dough to a ½-inch thickness. Cut with a 2-inch round cutter, or into 2-inch squares, and place on 2 ungreased baking sheets.
5. Bake at 400° for 12 to 15 minutes or until golden brown.

Try this twist!

Cinnamon-Raisin Angel Biscuits: Substitute ¼ cup firmly packed brown sugar for 2 Tbsp. sugar. Stir 1 cup baking raisins, 2 tsp. lemon zest, and 1 tsp. ground cinnamon into flour mixture in Step 2. Proceed with recipe as directed.

Note: We tested with Sun-Maid Baking Raisins.

PLAN AHEAD

Prepare recipe as directed through Step 3. Shape dough into a disk; refrigerate in a glass, airtight container up to 5 days. Let stand at room temperature 5 minutes. Roll, cut, and bake as directed in Steps 4 and 5. Unbaked biscuits may be frozen on a baking sheet, covered with plastic wrap, for 2 hours. Transfer frozen biscuits to a zip-top plastic freezer bag. Freeze up to 1 month. Let stand at room temperature 30 minutes before baking as directed.

CORNBREAD BISCUITS

*Add your own signature spin with a few
teaspoons of thyme, rosemary, or other favorite herb.*

MAKES: about 15 biscuits ▪ **HANDS-ON TIME:** 30 min. ▪ **TOTAL TIME:** 53 min.

3   cups self-rising soft-wheat flour
½   cup yellow self-rising
      cornmeal mix
¼   cup cold butter, cut into pieces
¼   cup shortening, cut into pieces
1½   cups buttermilk
1   tsp. yellow cornmeal
2   Tbsp. butter, melted

1. Preheat oven to 500°. Whisk together first 2 ingredients in a large bowl. Cut in cold butter and shortening with a pastry blender until mixture resembles small peas and dough is crumbly. Cover and chill 10 minutes. Add buttermilk, stirring just until dry ingredients are moistened.

2. Turn dough out onto a heavily floured surface; knead 3 or 4 times. Pat dough into a ¾-inch-thick circle.

3. Cut dough with a well-floured 2½-inch round cutter, rerolling scraps as needed. Sprinkle cornmeal on ungreased baking sheets; place biscuits on baking sheets. Lightly brush tops with 2 tbsp. melted butter.

4. Bake at 500° for 13 to 15 minutes or until golden brown.

Note: We tested with White Lily Bleached Self-Rising Flour.

UP-A-NOTCH SAUSAGE AND GRAVY

MAKES: 3 cups ▪ **HANDS-ON TIME:** 30 min. ▪ **TOTAL TIME:** 30 min.

½   (1-lb.) package mild ground
      pork sausage
Butter, melted (optional)
1   (4-oz.) package fresh shiitake
      mushrooms, stemmed
      and sliced
2   shallots, minced
¼   cup all-purpose flour
½   cup chicken broth
¼   cup dry sherry or white wine
2   cups half-and-half
2   Tbsp. chopped fresh parsley
1   Tbsp. chopped fresh sage
1   tsp. Worcestershire sauce
½   tsp. table salt
½   tsp. freshly ground black pepper

1. Cook sausage in a large heavy skillet over medium-high heat, stirring often, 3 to 5 minutes or until sausage crumbles and is no longer pink; drain, reserving ¼ cup sausage drippings in skillet. (If necessary, add melted butter to drippings to equal ¼ cup.)

2. Sauté mushrooms and shallots in hot drippings over medium-high heat 4 to 5 minutes or until golden. Whisk flour into mushroom mixture, and cook over medium-high heat, whisking constantly, 1 minute or until lightly browned. Add chicken broth and sherry, and cook 2 minutes, stirring to loosen browned bits from bottom of skillet. Stir in sausage.

3. Gradually add half-and-half, and cook over medium heat, stirring constantly, 2 to 3 minutes or until thickened and bubbly. Stir in parsley and next 4 ingredients. Reduce heat to low, and cook, stirring occasionally, 5 minutes. Serve warm.

UP-A-NOTCH SAUSAGE
AND GRAVY

SPICED PEACH-CARROT BREAD

MAKES: 1 loaf ▪ **HANDS-ON TIME:** 15 min. ▪ **TOTAL TIME:** 2 hours, 25 min.

2½ cups all-purpose flour
1 cup sugar
1 tsp. ground cinnamon
¾ tsp. baking soda
½ tsp. baking powder
½ tsp. table salt
¼ tsp. ground nutmeg
1½ cups peeled and chopped
  peaches
¾ cup freshly grated carrots
⅔ cup vegetable oil
½ cup milk
2 large eggs, lightly beaten
¾ cup toasted chopped pecans

1. Preheat oven to 350°.

2. Stir together flour and next 6 ingredients in a large bowl; add peaches and remaining ingredients, stirring just until dry ingredients are moistened. Spoon batter into a lightly greased 9- x 5-inch loaf pan.

3. Bake at 350° for 1 hour and 5 minutes to 1 hour and 10 minutes or until a wooden pick inserted in center comes out clean. Cool in pan on a wire rack 5 minutes. Remove from pan to wire rack, and cool completely (about 1 hour).

BREAKFAST

Make the morning magical with egg casseroles, pancakes, and other favorites that everyone will love.

FRIED EGG
SANDWICHES

FRIED EGG SANDWICHES

MAKES: 4 servings ▪ HANDS-ON TIME: 25 min. ▪ TOTAL TIME: 27 min.

4 (½-inch-thick) challah bread
  slices
2 Tbsp. butter, melted
1 (0.9-oz.) envelope hollandaise
  sauce mix
¼ tsp. lemon zest
1½ tsp. fresh lemon juice, divided
2 cups loosely packed arugula
½ cup loosely packed fresh flat-leaf
  parsley leaves
¼ cup thinly sliced red onion
3 tsp. extra virgin olive oil, divided
4 large eggs
¼ tsp. kosher salt
¼ tsp. freshly ground black pepper
12 thin pancetta slices, cooked
2 Tbsp. chopped sun-dried
  tomatoes

1. Preheat broiler with oven rack 5 to 6 inches from heat. Brush both sides of bread with butter; place on an aluminum foil-lined broiler pan. Broil 1 to 2 minutes on each side or until lightly toasted.

2. Prepare hollandaise sauce according to package directions; stir in zest and ½ tsp. lemon juice. Keep warm.

3. Toss together arugula, parsley, onion, 2 tsp. olive oil, and remaining 1 tsp. lemon juice.

4. Heat remaining 1 tsp. olive oil in a large nonstick skillet over medium heat. Gently break eggs into hot skillet; sprinkle with salt and black pepper. Cook 2 to 3 minutes on each side or to desired degree of doneness.

5. Top bread slices with arugula mixture, pancetta slices, and fried eggs. Spoon hollandaise sauce over each egg, and sprinkle with tomatoes. Serve immediately.

SAUSAGE-EGG ROLLUPS

MAKES: 6 servings ▪ HANDS-ON TIME: 15 min. ▪ TOTAL TIME: 15 min.

½ lb. ground pork sausage
1 Tbsp. olive oil
5 large eggs
1 Tbsp. milk
Pinch of table salt
Pinch of black pepper
¾ cup (3 oz.) shredded sharp
  Cheddar cheese
½ cup salsa
6 (6-inch) fajita-size flour tortillas

1. Cook sausage in hot oil in a large nonstick skillet over medium-high heat 4 to 5 minutes or until browned; drain.

2. Whisk together eggs and next 3 ingredients in a large bowl.

3. Add egg mixture to skillet, and cook over medium-high heat, without stirring, 2 to 3 minutes or until eggs begin to set on bottom. Gently draw cooked edges away from sides of skillet to form large pieces. Cook, stirring occasionally, 4 to 5 minutes or until eggs are thickened and moist. (Do not overstir.)

4. Divide sausage, scrambled eggs, cheese, and salsa equally among tortillas, spooning ingredients down center of each tortilla. Roll up tortillas.

CREAMY EGG STRATA

MAKES: 8 to 10 servings ▪ **HANDS-ON TIME:** 35 min. ▪ **TOTAL TIME:** 10 hours, 10 min.

½ (16-oz.) *French bread loaf, cubed (about 5 cups)*

6 *Tbsp. butter, divided*

2 *cups (8 oz.) shredded Swiss cheese*

½ *cup freshly grated Parmesan cheese*

⅓ *cup chopped onion*

1 *tsp. minced garlic*

3 *Tbsp. all-purpose flour*

1½ *cups chicken broth*

¾ *cup dry white wine*

½ *tsp. table salt*

½ *tsp. freshly ground black pepper*

¼ *tsp. ground nutmeg*

½ *cup sour cream*

8 *large eggs, lightly beaten*

Garnish: chopped fresh chives

1. Place bread cubes in a well-buttered 13- x 9-inch baking dish. Melt 3 Tbsp. butter, and drizzle over bread cubes. Sprinkle with cheeses.

2. Melt remaining 3 Tbsp. butter in a medium saucepan over medium heat; add onion and garlic. Sauté 2 to 3 minutes or until tender. Whisk in flour until smooth; cook, whisking constantly, 2 to 3 minutes or until lightly browned. Whisk in broth and next 4 ingredients until blended. Bring mixture to a boil; reduce heat to medium-low, and simmer, stirring occasionally, 15 minutes or until thickened. Remove from heat. Stir in sour cream. Add additional salt and pepper to taste.

3. Gradually whisk about one-fourth of hot sour cream mixture into eggs; add egg mixture to remaining sour cream mixture, whisking constantly. Pour mixture over cheeses in baking dish. Cover with plastic wrap, and chill 8 to 24 hours.

4. Let strata stand at room temperature 1 hour. Preheat oven to 350°. Remove plastic wrap, and bake 30 minutes or until set. Serve immediately.

PLAN AHEAD

Prepare this recipe Christmas Eve morning and chill overnight so that all you have to do Christmas morning is put the casserole in the oven while you enjoy opening gifts with family.

CARAMELIZED ONION
QUICHE

CARAMELIZED ONION QUICHE

MAKES: 6 to 8 servings ▪ **HANDS-ON TIME:** 45 min. ▪ **TOTAL TIME:** 2 hours

1   (14.1-oz.) package refrigerated piecrusts
3   large sweet onions, sliced (about 1½ lb.)
2   Tbsp. olive oil
½   cup chopped fresh flat-leaf parsley
6   cooked bacon slices, crumbled
2   cups (8 oz.) shredded Gruyère cheese
1½ cups half-and-half
4   large eggs
½   tsp. table salt
¼   tsp. freshly ground black pepper
¼   tsp. ground nutmeg
Garnish: additional chopped fresh parsley, chives

1. Preheat oven to 425°. Unroll piecrusts; stack on a lightly greased surface. Roll stacked piecrusts into a 12-inch circle. Fit piecrust into a 10-inch deep-dish tart pan with removable bottom; press into fluted edges. Trim off excess piecrust along edges. Line piecrust with aluminum foil and fill with pie weights or dried beans. Place pan on a foil-lined baking sheet. Bake 12 minutes. Remove weights and foil, and bake 8 more minutes. Cool completely on baking sheet on a wire rack (about 15 minutes). Reduce oven temperature to 350°.

2. Meanwhile, cook onions in hot oil in a large skillet over medium-high heat, stirring often, 15 to 20 minutes or until onions are caramel colored. Remove from heat, and stir in parsley and bacon. Place half of onion mixture in tart shell, and top with half of cheese; repeat with remaining onion mixture and cheese.

3. Whisk together half-and-half and next 4 ingredients; pour over cheese.

4. Bake at 350° for 40 to 45 minutes or until set. Cool on baking sheet on a wire rack 15 minutes before serving.

ASPARAGUS FRITTATA

MAKES: 6 servings ▪ **HANDS-ON TIME:** 30 min. ▪ **TOTAL TIME:** 30 min.

1   lb. fresh thin asparagus
2   Tbsp. butter
1   small onion, coarsely chopped
1   garlic clove, minced
12 large eggs
½   cup sour cream
¾   tsp. freshly ground black pepper
½   tsp. kosher salt
1   cup (4 oz.) shredded Gouda cheese
¼   cup freshly grated Parmesan cheese

1. Preheat oven to 350° with oven rack 6 inches from top of heat source. Snap off and discard tough ends of asparagus. Cut asparagus diagonally into 1-inch pieces. Melt butter in a 10-inch ovenproof skillet over medium-high heat. Add onion; sauté 3 to 4 minutes or until tender. Add asparagus; sauté 3 to 4 minutes or until tender. Add garlic, and sauté 1 minute.

2. Whisk together eggs and next 3 ingredients until well blended. Stir in ¾ cup Gouda cheese. Fold egg mixture into vegetable mixture in skillet. Cook, stirring occasionally, 2 to 3 minutes or until almost set. Sprinkle with Parmesan cheese and remaining ¼ cup Gouda cheese.

3. Bake at 350° for 5 minutes or until set. Increase oven temperature to broil, and broil 3 to 4 minutes or until golden brown.

GRITS-AND-GREENS BREAKFAST BAKE

Give yourself a head start: Make Simple Collard Greens up to three days ahead.

MAKES: 8 servings ▪ **HANDS-ON TIME:** 25 min. ▪ **TOTAL TIME:** 2 hours, 7 min., including collard greens

1   tsp. table salt
1½ cups uncooked quick-cooking
        grits
1   cup (4 oz.) shredded white
        Cheddar cheese
3   Tbsp. butter
½   cup half-and-half
¼   tsp. freshly ground black pepper
¼   tsp. ground red pepper
2   large eggs
3   cups Simple Collard Greens,
        drained
8   large eggs
Hot sauce (optional)

1. Preheat oven to 375°. Bring table salt and 4 cups water to a boil in a large saucepan over medium-high heat; gradually whisk in grits. Reduce heat to medium, and cook, whisking often, 5 to 7 minutes or until thickened. Remove from heat, and stir in cheese and butter.

2. Whisk together half-and-half, black pepper, red pepper, and 2 eggs in a medium bowl. Stir half-and-half mixture into grits mixture. Stir in Simple Collard Greens. Pour mixture into a lightly greased 13- x 9-inch baking dish.

3. Bake at 375° for 25 to 30 minutes or until set. Remove from oven.

4. Make 8 indentations in grits mixture with back of a large spoon. Break remaining 8 eggs, 1 at a time, and slip 1 egg into each indentation. Bake 12 to 14 minutes or until eggs are cooked to desired degree of doneness. Cover loosely with aluminum foil, and let stand 10 minutes. Serve with hot sauce, if desired.

Simple Collard Greens

MAKES: 3 cups ▪ **HANDS-ON TIME:** 10 min. ▪ **TOTAL TIME:** 50 min.

½   medium-size sweet onion,
        chopped
2   Tbsp. olive oil
1   (16-oz.) package fresh collard
        greens, washed, trimmed, and
        chopped
1½ tsp. table salt

Cook onion in hot oil in a large Dutch oven over medium heat, stirring occasionally, 10 minutes or until tender. Add collard greens, salt, and 3 cups water. Bring to a boil; reduce heat, and simmer 30 minutes or until tender.

SLOW-COOKER GRITS

Simplify your morning: Soak the grits the night before.

MAKES: 8 servings ▪ **HANDS-ON TIME:** 10 min. ▪ **TOTAL TIME:** 10 hours, 10 min.

2 cups uncooked stone-ground
    grits
¼ cup heavy cream
2 Tbsp. butter
1½ tsp. table salt
½ tsp. black pepper
Toppings: boiled shrimp,
    shredded Cheddar cheese,
    sliced smoked sausage,
    chopped green onion,
    chopped chives

1. Stir together grits and 6 cups water in a 5- or 6-qt. slow cooker. Let stand 1 to 2 minutes, allowing grits to settle to bottom. Tilt cooker slightly; skim off solids using a fine wire-mesh strainer. Cover; soak 8 hours or overnight.
2. Cover and cook grits on HIGH 2 hours to 2 hours and 30 minutes, stirring halfway through. Stir in cream and next 3 ingredients. Serve with desired toppings.

Create a Grits Bar

Offer these toppings with a few staples.

Bourbon Mushrooms: Melt ¼ cup butter with ¼ cup olive oil in a large skillet over medium heat; add 2 lb. sliced assorted fresh mushrooms, ¾ tsp. salt, and ¼ tsp. black pepper. Cook, stirring occasionally, 12 to 15 minutes or until tender and almost all liquid has evaporated. Remove from heat. Stir in ½ cup bourbon or chicken broth; return to heat, and cook 2 to 3 minutes or until slightly thickened. Reduce heat to low; stir in 3 garlic cloves, minced; 2 Tbsp. chopped fresh parsley; and 1 Tbsp. chopped fresh thyme. Cook 1 more minute. Makes: 8 to 10 servings.

Easy Creole Sauce: Sauté 2 celery ribs, chopped, in 2 Tbsp. olive oil in a saucepan over medium heat 3 to 4 minutes until tender. Stir in 2 (14.5-oz.) cans diced tomatoes with green peppers and onion; 3 garlic cloves, minced; 2 tsp. Creole seasoning; and 1 tsp. sugar. Reduce heat to low; simmer, stirring occasionally, 20 minutes. Stir in 2 Tbsp. chopped fresh flat-leaf parsley; 2 green onions, thinly sliced; and 1 tsp. hot sauce. Store in refrigerator up to 2 days. Makes: 3 cups.

Great Grits Combos
Boiled Shrimp + Easy Creole Sauce
Bourbon Mushrooms + Spinach + Swiss + Bacon
Chopped Ham + Shredded Cheddar
Caramelized Onions + Shredded Smoked Gruyère
Shredded Barbecued Pork + BBQ Sauce + Sautéed Spinach

MINI GRITS AND GREENS

Warm ceramic soup spoons in a 200° oven for 10 minutes before assembling.

MAKES: 3 dozen ▪ **HANDS-ON TIME:** 25 min. ▪ **TOTAL TIME:** 45 min.

1   cup chicken broth
⅓   cup half-and-half
¼   tsp. table salt
½   cup uncooked regular grits
½   cup (2 oz.) freshly shredded
      Cheddar cheese
¼   cup freshly grated Parmesan
      cheese
1   Tbsp. butter
½   tsp. hot sauce
¼   tsp. freshly ground black pepper
8   large fresh collard green leaves
2   small dry Spanish chorizo
      sausage links (about 2¾ oz.)
1   Tbsp. olive oil
2   tsp. apple cider vinegar
½   tsp. sugar
36   porcelain tasting spoons,
      warmed
Garnish: chopped fresh chives

1. Bring first 3 ingredients and 1 cup water to a boil in a medium saucepan over high heat; gradually whisk in grits. Cover, reduce heat to medium-low, and simmer, stirring occasionally, 15 minutes or until thickened. Whisk in Cheddar cheese and next 4 ingredients, whisking constantly until cheese melts. Keep warm.

2. Rinse collard greens. Trim and discard thick stems from bottom of collard green leaves (about 2 inches). Stack collard greens on a cutting board. Tightly roll up leaves, and thinly slice into ⅛-inch strips. Quarter chorizo lengthwise, and cut into small pieces.

3. Sauté chorizo in hot oil in a large skillet over medium-high heat 2 minutes. Add collard greens, vinegar, and sugar. Cook, stirring constantly, 2 minutes or until greens are bright green and just tender. Season with additional salt and pepper to taste.

4. Place about 1 Tbsp. grits onto each warm spoon, and top with collard mixture. Serve immediately.

Note: *We tested with Quijote Chorizos Caseros Home-Style Dry Sausage.*

CRACKER SPOONS
with Pimiento Cheese

MAKES: 5 dozen ▪ **HANDS-ON TIME:** 25 min. ▪ **TOTAL TIME:** 1 Hour, 20 min., including pimiento cheese

1½   (14.1-oz.) packages refrigerated
      piecrusts
1   egg white, beaten
¾   tsp. seasoned salt
Parchment paper
Pimiento cheese
Garnishes: diced pimiento,
      chopped fresh chives

1. Preheat oven to 400°. Unroll piecrusts; brush with egg white, and sprinkle with seasoned salt (about ¼ tsp. per crust). Cut dough into rounds using a 4½- or 5-inch teaspoon-shaped cutter. Place cutouts 1 inch apart on parchment paper-lined baking sheets.

2. Bake, in batches, at 400° for 9 to 11 minutes or until lightly browned and crisp. Remove from baking sheets to a wire rack, and cool completely (about 20 minutes). Store in an airtight container 1 day, or freeze up to 2 weeks.

3. Spoon pimiento cheese into a zip-top plastic freezer bag. (Do not seal.) Snip 1 corner of bag to make a small hole. Pipe pimiento cheese onto end of each spoon.

MINI GRITS AND GREENS

CRACKER SPOONS WITH
PIMIENTO CHEESE

GEORGIA GRITS WAFFLES

MAKES: 8 servings ▪ **HANDS-ON TIME:** 25 min. ▪ **TOTAL TIME:** 50 min., not including toppings

½ cup uncooked regular grits
6 Tbsp. cold unsalted butter, cubed
2 large eggs, lightly beaten
¾ cup buttermilk
1¼ cups all-purpose flour
1 Tbsp. sugar
2 tsp. baking powder
½ tsp. baking soda
Toppings: Vanilla Crème Anglaise
(optional), Maple-Bacon
Praline Syrup (optional)

1. Bring 2 cups water to a boil over medium-high heat in a medium saucepan. Whisk in grits; bring to a boil. Reduce heat to low; cook, stirring often, 15 minutes or until tender. Stir in butter until melted; cool to room temperature. Stir in eggs and buttermilk.

2. Whisk together flour and next 3 ingredients in a small bowl. Stir flour mixture into grits mixture until just combined.

3. Cook in a preheated, oiled waffle iron until golden (about ⅓ cup batter each). Remove from iron. Serve with Vanilla Crème Anglaise and Maple-Bacon Praline Syrup, if desired.

Vanilla Crème Anglaise

MAKES: 1 cup ▪ **HANDS-ON TIME:** 20 min. ▪ **TOTAL TIME:** 20 min.

½ cup 2% reduced-fat milk
½ cup heavy cream
3 egg yolks
¼ cup sugar
Pinch of kosher salt
½ tsp. vanilla extract

1. Heat milk and cream in a heavy saucepan over medium-low heat just until bubbles and steam appear (do not boil).

2. Reduce heat to low. Whisk together egg yolks, and next 2 ingredients in a bowl; gradually whisk in one-fourth of hot milk mixture. Gradually add warm egg mixture to remaining hot milk mixture, whisking constantly; cook, whisking constantly, 7 minutes or until mixture thinly coats the back of a wooden spoon. Remove from heat. Whisk in vanilla.

3. Pour through a fine wire-mesh strainer into a large bowl. Serve warm.

Maple-Bacon Praline Syrup

½ cup butter
½ cup chopped pecans
½ cup pure maple syrup
2 thick hickory-smoked bacon
slices, cooked and crumbled

Cook all ingredients in a saucepan over medium-low heat, stirring often, 5 minutes or until blended.

ITALIAN CREAM PANCAKES

MAKES: about 18 pancakes ▪ **HANDS-ON TIME:** 35 min. ▪ **TOTAL TIME:** 50 min., including syrup

2 cups all-purpose flour

⅓ cup sugar

1 tsp. baking powder

½ tsp. baking soda

½ tsp. table salt

1 cup buttermilk

¾ cup heavy cream

2 Tbsp. butter, melted

2 tsp. vanilla extract

2 large eggs, separated

⅔ cup finely chopped toasted pecans

½ cup sweetened flaked coconut

Cream Cheese Syrup

Garnish: chopped toasted pecans

1. Stir together flour and next 4 ingredients in a large bowl. Whisk together buttermilk, next 3 ingredients, and 2 egg yolks in another bowl. Gradually stir buttermilk mixture into flour mixture just until dry ingredients are moistened. Stir in toasted pecans and coconut. Beat egg whites at high speed with an electric mixer until stiff peaks form; fold into batter.

2. Pour about ¼ cup batter for each pancake onto a hot buttered griddle or large nonstick skillet. Cook pancakes over medium heat 3 to 4 minutes or until tops are covered with bubbles and edges look dry and cooked. Turn and cook 3 to 4 minutes or until done. (Keep pancakes warm in a 200° oven up to 30 minutes.) Stack pancakes on individual plates. Serve with Cream Cheese Syrup.

Cream Cheese Syrup

MAKES: 1 ¼ cups ▪ **HANDS-ON TIME:** 10 min. ▪ **TOTAL TIME:** 10 min.

½ (8-oz.) package cream cheese, softened

¼ cup butter, softened

¼ cup maple syrup

1 tsp. vanilla extract

1 cup powdered sugar

¼ cup milk

Beat first 4 ingredients at medium speed with an electric mixer until creamy. Gradually add sugar, beating until smooth. Gradually add milk, beating until smooth. If desired, microwave in a microwave-safe bowl at HIGH 10 to 15 seconds or just until warm; stir until smooth.

GERMAN CHOCOLATE PANCAKES

MAKES: about 20 pancakes ▪ **HANDS-ON TIME:** 35 min. ▪ **TOTAL TIME:** 55 min., including syrup

2   cups all-purpose flour
½   cup sugar
½   cup unsweetened cocoa
1½   Tbsp. baking powder
1   tsp. table salt
2   cups milk
2   large eggs, lightly beaten
½   (4-oz.) sweet chocolate baking
       bar, finely chopped
3   Tbsp. butter, melted
1   tsp. vanilla extract
German Chocolate Syrup
Garnishes: chocolate curls, white
       chocolate curls

1. Whisk together first 5 ingredients in a large bowl. Whisk together milk and next 4 ingredients in another bowl. Gradually stir milk mixture into flour mixture just until moistened.

2. Pour about ¼ cup batter for each pancake onto a hot buttered griddle or large nonstick skillet. Cook pancakes over medium heat 3 to 4 minutes or until tops are covered with bubbles and edges look dry and cooked. Turn and cook 3 to 4 minutes or until done. (Keep pancakes warm in a 200° oven up to 30 minutes.) Stack pancakes on individual plates. Serve with German Chocolate Syrup.

German Chocolate Syrup

MAKES: 1 ½ cups ▪ **HANDS-ON TIME:** 15 min. ▪ **TOTAL TIME:** 20 min.

⅔   cup chopped pecans
⅔   cup sweetened flaked coconut
1   (5-oz.) can evaporated milk
2   egg yolks, lightly beaten
½   cup firmly packed light brown
       sugar
¼   cup butter, melted
½   tsp. vanilla extract

1. Preheat oven to 350°. Bake pecans and coconut in a single layer in a shallow pan 5 to 7 minutes or until lightly toasted and fragrant, stirring halfway through.

2. Cook evaporated milk and next 3 ingredients in a heavy 2-qt. saucepan over medium heat, stirring constantly, 8 to 10 minutes or until mixture bubbles and begins to thicken. Remove from heat, and stir in vanilla, pecans, and coconut. Serve immediately, or store in an airtight container in refrigerator up to 1 week.

Tip: To reheat, microwave syrup in a microwave-safe bowl at HIGH 10 to 15 seconds or just until warm; stir until smooth.

CREAM CHEESE-FILLED WREATH

MAKES: 10 to 12 servings ▪ HANDS-ON TIME: 30 min. ▪ TOTAL TIME: 10 hours, 15 min., including filling and glaze

1   (8-oz.) container sour cream
½ cup sugar
½ cup butter, cut up
1   tsp. table salt
2   (¼-oz.) envelopes active dry
     yeast
½ cup warm water (105° to 115°)
2   tsp. sugar
2   large eggs, lightly beaten
4   cups bread flour
Cream Cheese Filling
Vanilla Glaze
Garnish: sparkling sugar

1. Cook first 4 ingredients in a small saucepan over medium-low heat, stirring occasionally, 5 minutes or until butter melts. Cool until an instant-read thermometer registers 105° to 115° (about 10 minutes).

2. Combine yeast, warm water, and 2 tsp. sugar in a large bowl; let stand 5 minutes. Stir in sour cream mixture and eggs; gradually stir in flour. (Dough will be soft.) Cover and chill 8 to 24 hours.

3. Turn dough out onto a heavily floured surface; knead 4 or 5 times. Roll dough into a 24- x 8-inch rectangle; spread with Cream Cheese Filling, leaving a 1-inch border around edges. Roll up dough, jelly-roll fashion, starting at 1 long side; press seam. Place, seam side down, on a lightly greased baking sheet. Bring ends of roll together to form a ring; moisten and pinch edges to seal. Cover; let rise in a warm place (85°), free from drafts, 1 hour or until doubled in bulk.

4. Preheat oven to 375°. Bake 20 to 22 minutes or until browned. Transfer to a serving plate. Drizzle with Vanilla Glaze.

Cream Cheese Filling

MAKES: 2 cups ▪ HANDS-ON TIME: 5 min. ▪ TOTAL TIME: 5 min.

2   (8-oz.) packages cream cheese,
     softened
½ cup sugar
1   large egg
2   tsp. vanilla extract

Beat all ingredients at medium speed with an electric mixer until smooth.

Vanilla Glaze

MAKES: about 1 cup ▪ HANDS-ON TIME: 5 min. ▪ TOTAL TIME: 5 min.

2½ cups powdered sugar
¼ cup milk
2   tsp. vanilla extract

Stir together all ingredients in a small bowl until blended.

OVERNIGHT COFFEE CRUMBLE CAKE

MAKES: 8 to 10 servings ▪ **HANDS-ON TIME:** 20 min. ▪ **TOTAL TIME:** 9 hours, 7 min., including crumble and drizzle

¾ cup butter, softened
1 cup sugar
2 large eggs
2 cups all-purpose flour
1 tsp. baking powder
1 tsp. baking soda
½ tsp. table salt
1 cup buttermilk
1 tsp. vanilla extract
Cinnamon-Nut Crumble
Sweet Bourbon Drizzle

1. Beat butter at medium speed with an electric mixer until creamy; gradually add sugar, beating well. Add eggs, 1 at a time, beating just until blended after each addition.

2. Combine flour and next 3 ingredients in a medium bowl. Add flour mixture to butter mixture alternately with buttermilk, beginning and ending with flour mixture. Stir in vanilla. Pour batter into a greased and floured 13- x 9-inch pan. Cover tightly, and chill 8 to 24 hours.

3. Preheat oven to 350°. Let cake stand at room temperature 30 minutes. Sprinkle with Cinnamon-Nut Crumble. Bake 32 to 35 minutes or until wooden pick inserted in center comes out clean. Transfer to a serving plate; drizzle with Sweet Bourbon Drizzle.

Cinnamon-Nut Crumble

MAKES: 2 cups ▪ **HANDS-ON TIME:** 10 min. ▪ **TOTAL TIME:** 10 min.

½ cup coarsely chopped pecans
¼ cup coarsely chopped walnuts
½ cup slivered almonds
½ cup firmly packed brown sugar
6 Tbsp. all-purpose flour
3 Tbsp. butter, melted
1 tsp. ground cinnamon

Stir together all ingredients in a medium bowl.

Sweet Bourbon Drizzle

MAKES: 1 cup ▪ **HANDS-ON TIME:** 5 min. ▪ **TOTAL TIME:** 5 min.

2 cups powdered sugar
1 Tbsp. bourbon
2 to 3 Tbsp. milk

Stir together powdered sugar, bourbon, and 2 Tbsp. milk in a small bowl. Stir in remaining 1 Tbsp. milk, 1 tsp. at a time, until desired consistency. Use immediately.

SWEET POTATO COFFEE CAKE

MAKES: 10 to 12 servings ▪ **HANDS-ON TIME:** 30 min. ▪ **TOTAL TIME:** 3 hours, including glaze

2   (¼-oz.) envelopes active dry yeast
½   cup warm water (105° to 115°)
1   tsp. granulated sugar
5½ cups bread flour, divided
1½ tsp. table salt
1   tsp. baking soda
1   cup cooked mashed sweet potato
1   large egg, lightly beaten
1   cup buttermilk
½   cup granulated sugar
¼   cup butter, melted
1   Tbsp. orange zest
⅔   cup granulated sugar
⅔   cup firmly packed brown sugar
1   Tbsp. ground cinnamon
¼   cup butter, melted
Caramel Glaze

1. Stir together first 3 ingredients in a 1-cup glass measuring cup; let stand 5 minutes.
2. Stir together 4½ cups bread flour, salt, and baking soda.
3. Beat yeast mixture and ½ cup bread flour at medium speed with a heavy-duty electric stand mixer until well blended. Gradually add sweet potato, next 5 ingredients, and flour mixture, beating until well blended.
4. Turn dough out onto a well-floured surface, and knead until smooth and elastic (about 4 to 5 minutes), gradually adding remaining ½ cup bread flour. Place dough in a lightly greased large bowl, turning to grease top. Cover and let rise in a warm place (85°), free from drafts, 1 to 1½ hours or until doubled in bulk.
5. Stir together ⅔ cup granulated sugar, brown sugar, and cinnamon. Punch dough down; turn out onto a well-floured surface. Divide dough in half. Roll 1 portion into a 16- x 12-inch rectangle. Brush with half of ¼ cup melted butter. Sprinkle with half of sugar mixture. Cut dough lengthwise into 6 (2-inch-wide) strips using a pizza cutter or knife.
6. Loosely coil 1 strip, and place in center of a lightly greased 10-inch round pan. Loosely coil remaining dough strips, 1 at a time, around center strip, attaching each to the end of the previous strip to make a single large spiral. (Sugared sides of dough strips should face center of spiral.) Repeat with remaining dough half, butter, and sugar mixture.
7. Cover; let rise in a warm place (85°), free from drafts, 30 minutes or until doubled in bulk.
8. Preheat oven to 350°. Bake 30 minutes or until lightly browned and a wooden pick inserted in center comes out clean. Cool in pans on a wire rack 10 minutes. Remove from pans to serving plates. Prepare Caramel Glaze, and brush over swirls.

Caramel Glaze

MAKES: 1½ cups ▪ **HANDS-ON TIME:** 15 min. ▪ **TOTAL TIME:** 15 min.

1   cup firmly packed brown sugar
½   cup butter
¼   cup evaporated milk
1   cup powdered sugar, sifted
1   tsp. vanilla extract

Bring first 3 ingredients to a boil in a 2-qt. saucepan over medium heat, whisking constantly. Boil, whisking constantly, 1 minute. Remove from heat; whisk in powdered sugar and vanilla until smooth. Stir gently 3 to 5 minutes or until mixture begins to cool and slightly thickens. Use immediately.

LEMON-ROSEMARY COFFEE CAKE

MAKES: 8 to 10 servings ▪ **HANDS-ON TIME:** 25 min. ▪ **TOTAL TIME:** 2 hours, 20 min.

Parchment paper
3   large lemons
2   cups all-purpose flour
1¼ cups sugar
½   tsp. table salt
½   cup very cold butter, cubed
1   tsp. baking powder
½   tsp. baking soda
¾   cup buttermilk*
1   large egg
1½ tsp. chopped fresh rosemary
1   (10-oz.) jar lemon curd
Powdered sugar
Garnishes: fresh rosemary sprigs,
    lemon slices, lemon rind curls

1. Preheat oven to 350°. Lightly grease bottom and sides of a 9-inch springform pan**. Line bottom of pan with parchment paper.

2. Grate zest from lemons to equal 1 Tbsp. Cut lemons in half; squeeze juice from lemons into a bowl to equal 5 Tbsp. Reserve zest and 1 Tbsp. lemon juice.

3. Combine flour, sugar, and salt in bowl of a food processor; pulse 3 to 4 times or until blended. Add butter; pulse 6 to 7 times or until mixture resembles coarse crumbs. Reserve 1 cup flour mixture.

4. Transfer remaining flour mixture to bowl of a heavy-duty electric stand mixer. Add baking powder and baking soda; beat at low speed until well blended. Add buttermilk, egg, and ¼ cup lemon juice; beat at medium speed 1½ to 2 minutes or until batter is thoroughly blended, stopping to scrape bowl as needed. Stir in rosemary. Spoon half of batter into prepared pan.

5. Whisk lemon curd in a small bowl about 1 minute or until loosened and smooth; carefully spread over batter in pan. Top with remaining half of batter.

6. Stir together reserved lemon zest, 1 Tbsp. lemon juice, and 1 cup flour mixture; sprinkle lemon zest mixture over batter in pan.

7. Bake at 350° for 45 to 50 minutes or until a long wooden pick inserted in center comes out clean.

8. Cool in pan on a wire rack 10 minutes. Gently run a sharp knife around edge of cake to loosen; remove sides of pan. Cool cake completely on wire rack (about 1 hour). Dust with powdered sugar just before serving.

*Greek yogurt may be substituted.
**A 9-inch round cake pan may be substituted for springform pan. Line bottom and sides of cake pan with aluminum foil, allowing 2 to 3 inches to extend over sides; grease foil well. Proceed with recipe as directed through Step 7. Cool in pan on a wire rack 10 minutes. Lift cake from pan, using foil sides as handles. Carefully remove foil. Cool; dust with powdered sugar as directed.

MINI BANANA-CRANBERRY-NUT BREAD LOAVES

Use bananas that appear to be past their prime for this recipe.

MAKES: 5 miniature loaves ▪ **HANDS-ON TIME:** 20 min. ▪ **TOTAL TIME:** 1 hour, 25 min., including glaze

1   (8-oz.) package cream cheese, softened
¾   cup butter, softened
2   cups sugar
2   large eggs
3   cups all-purpose flour
½   tsp. baking powder
½   tsp. baking soda
½   tsp. table salt
1½ cups mashed ripe bananas
¾   cup chopped fresh cranberries
½   tsp. vanilla extract
¾   cup chopped toasted pecans
Orange Glaze

1. Preheat oven to 350°. Beat cream cheese and butter at medium speed with an electric mixer until creamy. Gradually add sugar, beating until light and fluffy. Add eggs, 1 at a time, beating just until blended after each addition.

2. Combine flour and next 3 ingredients; gradually add to butter mixture, beating at low speed just until blended. Stir in bananas and next 3 ingredients. Spoon about 1½ cups batter into each of 5 greased and floured 5- x 3-inch miniature loaf pans.

3. Bake at 350° for 40 to 44 minutes or until a wooden pick inserted in center comes out clean and sides pull away from pans. Cool in pans 10 minutes. Transfer to wire racks. Prepare Orange Glaze. Drizzle over warm bread loaves, and cool 10 minutes.

Make Ahead: Freeze baked, unglazed loaves in zip-top plastic freezer bags. Thaw loaves at room temperature. Reheat loaves at 300° for 10 to 12 minutes. Drizzle with glaze.

Orange Glaze

MAKES: ½ cup ▪ **HANDS-ON TIME:** 5 min. ▪ **TOTAL TIME:** 5 min.

1   cup powdered sugar
1   tsp. orange zest
2 to 3 Tbsp. fresh orange juice

Stir together all ingredients in a small bowl until blended. Use immediately.

BLUEBERRY MUFFINS

MAKES: 1½ dozen ▪ **HANDS-ON TIME:** 15 min. ▪ **TOTAL TIME:** 40 min.

3½ cups all-purpose flour
1 cup sugar
1 Tbsp. baking powder
1½ tsp. table salt
3 large eggs
1½ cups milk
½ cup butter, melted
2 cups frozen blueberries
1 Tbsp. all-purpose flour
Lemon-Cream Cheese Glaze
    (optional)
Garnish: lemon zest

1. Preheat oven to 450°. Stir together first 4 ingredients. Whisk together eggs and next 2 ingredients; add to flour mixture, stirring just until dry ingredients are moistened. Toss blueberries with 1 Tbsp. flour, and gently fold into batter. Spoon mixture into 1½ lightly greased 12-cup muffin pans, filling three-fourths full.
2. Bake at 450° for 14 to 15 minutes or until lightly browned and a wooden pick inserted into center comes out clean. Immediately remove from pans to wire racks, and cool 10 minutes.
3. Meanwhile, prepare Lemon-Cream Cheese Glaze, and drizzle over warm muffins, if desired.

Fresh blueberries may be substituted for frozen blueberries.

Lemon-Cream Cheese Glaze

MAKES: ¾ cup ▪ **HANDS-ON TIME:** 10 min. ▪ **TOTAL TIME:** 10 min.

1 (3-oz.) package cream cheese, softened
1 tsp. lemon zest
1 Tbsp. fresh lemon juice
¼ tsp. vanilla extract
1½ cups sifted powdered sugar

Beat cream cheese at medium speed with an electric mixer until creamy. Add lemon zest, lemon juice, and vanilla; beat until smooth. Gradually add powdered sugar, beating until smooth.

OKRA-SHRIMP BEIGNETS

*We took two Lowcountry favorites, okra and shrimp, and fried them
into fritters that have the crispy and airy qualities of a good beignet, hence the name.*

MAKES: about 30 ▪ **HANDS-ON TIME:** 27 min. ▪ **TOTAL TIME:** 47 min., including salsa and sour cream

Peanut oil
2   cups sliced fresh okra
½   green bell pepper, diced
½   medium onion, diced
1   large egg
½   cup all-purpose flour
¼   cup heavy cream
1   jalapeño pepper, finely chopped
¾   tsp. salt
¼   tsp. freshly ground pepper
¼   lb. unpeeled, medium-size
      raw shrimp, peeled and
      coarsely chopped
Fresh Tomato Salsa
Cilantro Sour Cream

1. Pour oil to depth of 3 inches into a Dutch oven; heat to 350°.
2. Stir together okra and next 8 ingredients in a large bowl until well blended; stir in shrimp.
3. Drop batter by rounded tablespoonfuls into hot oil, and fry, in batches, 2 to 3 minutes on each side or until golden brown. Drain on a wire rack over paper towels. Serve with Fresh Tomato Salsa and Cilantro Sour Cream.

Fresh Tomato Salsa

MAKES: 4 servings ▪ **HANDS-ON TIME:** 15 min. ▪ **TOTAL TIME:** 15 min.

4   large plum tomatoes, seeded
      and chopped (about 2 cups)
¼   cup fresh cilantro, chopped
1   jalapeño pepper, seeded and
      finely diced
3   Tbsp. red onion, finely diced
2½ Tbsp. fresh lime juice
1   Tbsp. extra virgin olive oil

Stir together all ingredients. Add salt and pepper to taste; garnish with cilantro.

Cilantro Sour Cream

MAKES: 1 cup ▪ **HANDS-ON TIME:** 5 min. ▪ **TOTAL TIME:** 5 min.

1   (8-oz.) container sour cream
¼   cup fresh cilantro, chopped
1   tsp. lime zest
1   tsp. fresh lime juice

Stir together all ingredients. Add salt and pepper to taste.

GOUDA GRITS

GOUDA GRITS

MAKES: 8 servings ▪ **HANDS-ON TIME:** 10 min. ▪ **TOTAL TIME:** 30 min.

4 cups chicken broth
1 cup whipping cream
1 tsp. table salt
¼ tsp. freshly ground black pepper
2 cups uncooked quick-cooking grits
2 cups (8 oz.) shredded Gouda cheese
½ cup buttermilk
¼ cup butter
2 tsp. hot sauce
Garnishes: shredded Gouda cheese, chopped green onions, black pepper

Bring first 4 ingredients and 4 cups water to a boil in a Dutch oven over high heat; whisk in grits, reduce heat to medium-low, and simmer, stirring occasionally, 15 minutes or until thickened. Remove from heat, and stir in Gouda and next 3 ingredients.

SUNSHINE CITRUS PLATTER

MAKES: 8 servings ▪ **HANDS-ON TIME:** 20 min. ▪ **TOTAL TIME:** 1 hour, 20 min.

4 navel oranges
2 Ruby Red or Rio Star grapefruit
2 Tbsp. powdered sugar
Ground cinnamon

1. Peel oranges and grapefruit; cut into ½-inch-thick rounds. Cover and chill 1 to 24 hours.
2. Arrange fruit on a large platter. Sift powdered sugar over fruit; sprinkle with cinnamon. Serve immediately.

BROWN SUGAR-AND-CORNMEAL-CRUSTED BACON

For easy cleanup, line the jelly-roll pans with aluminum foil.

MAKES: 8 servings ▪ **HANDS-ON TIME:** 15 min. ▪ **TOTAL TIME:** 1 hour

¼ cup plain yellow cornmeal
3 Tbsp. brown sugar
1½ tsp. freshly ground black pepper
16 thick bacon slices

1. Preheat oven to 400°. Combine first 3 ingredients in a shallow dish. Dredge bacon slices in cornmeal mixture, shaking off excess.

2. Place half of bacon in a single layer on a lightly greased wire rack in a jelly-roll pan. Place remaining bacon in a single layer on another lightly greased wire rack in a second jelly-roll pan.

3. Bake at 400° for 40 to 45 minutes or until browned and crisp. Cool 5 minutes.

SECOND HELPINGS

Rethink your leftovers! We upgraded the iconic day-after sandwich with some fresh alternatives.

SWEET POTATO SOUP

Make the soup through Step 2 the day before.
Reheat and stir in the lime juice before serving.

MAKES: 8 cups ▪ **HANDS-ON TIME:** 35 min. ▪ **TOTAL TIME:** 1 hour

2   Tbsp. butter
1   medium-size onion, chopped
2   garlic cloves, minced
5½ cups reduced-sodium fat-free
      chicken broth
2   lb. sweet potatoes, peeled and
      chopped (2 large)
1   cup apple cider
1   tsp. table salt
1   tsp. minced canned chipotle
      pepper in adobo sauce
2   Tbsp. fresh lime juice
½   cup sour cream
2   tsp. fresh lime juice
Garnishes: fresh parsley leaves,
      smoked paprika

1. Melt butter in a large saucepan over medium-high heat; add onion, and sauté 5 to 7 minutes or until tender. Add garlic; sauté 1 minute. Stir in broth and next 4 ingredients. Bring to a boil; reduce heat to medium-low, and simmer 20 minutes or until potatoes are tender.

2. Process mixture with a handheld blender until smooth. (If you don't have a handheld blender, cool mixture 10 minutes, and process, in batches, in a regular blender until smooth. Return to saucepan, and proceed with Step 3.)

3. Cook potato mixture over low heat, stirring occasionally, 5 minutes or until thoroughly heated. Stir in 2 Tbsp. lime juice. Whisk together sour cream and 2 tsp. lime juice. Ladle soup into bowls, and drizzle each serving with sour cream mixture.

BUTTERNUT SQUASH SOUP

MAKES: 10½ cups ▪ **HANDS-ON TIME:** 30 min. ▪ **TOTAL TIME:** 1 hour, 10 min.

2   carrots, cut into 1-inch pieces
1   sweet onion, chopped
3   Tbsp. olive oil
1   (3-lb.) butternut squash, peeled
      and cut into 1-inch pieces
6   cups chicken broth
1   tsp. orange zest
1   cup heavy cream
3   Tbsp. white wine vinegar
1   Tbsp. orange blossom honey
¾   tsp. kosher salt
½   tsp. freshly ground white pepper
½   tsp. hot sauce

1. Sauté carrots and onion in hot olive oil in a Dutch oven over medium-high heat 8 to 10 minutes or until lightly browned. Add squash, broth, and orange zest; bring to a boil. Cover, reduce heat to medium, and simmer 20 to 25 minutes or until squash is tender. Stir in cream and next 5 ingredients. Cool slightly (about 10 minutes).

2. Process mixture with a handheld blender until smooth. (If you don't have a handheld blender, cool mixture 10 minutes, and process, in batches, in a regular blender until smooth.) Serve warm.

TORTILLA TURKEY SOUP

MAKES: 8 cups ▪ HANDS-ON TIME: 30 min. ▪ TOTAL TIME: 40 min.

10 (6-inch) fajita-size corn tortillas, cut into ½-inch-wide strips, divided
Vegetable cooking spray
1 small onion, chopped
2 garlic cloves, chopped
1 small jalapeño pepper, seeded and minced
1 Tbsp. olive oil
1 (32-oz.) container chicken broth
1 (10-oz.) can medium enchilada sauce
2 cups chopped cooked turkey
1 tsp. ground cumin
Toppings: chopped avocado, shredded sharp Cheddar cheese, chopped fresh cilantro, chopped tomatoes

1. Preheat oven to 450°. Place 5 tortilla strips in a single layer on a baking sheet. Coat strips with cooking spray; bake 10 minutes or until browned and crisp, stirring once.

2. Sauté onion and next 2 ingredients in hot olive oil in a Dutch oven over medium-high heat 5 to 6 minutes or until browned.

3. Add chicken broth and remaining unbaked tortilla strips to onion mixture. Cook broth mixture over medium heat 3 to 5 minutes or until tortilla strips soften and broth mixture slightly thickens.

4. Stir in enchilada sauce and next 2 ingredients, and cook 6 to 8 minutes or until mixture is thoroughly heated. (Do not boil.) Serve with baked tortilla strips and desired toppings.

HOLIDAY TRADITION

Complete the meal with a delicious salad such as the Crispy Goat Cheese-Topped Arugula Salad (page 65) or the Fresh Pear-and-Green Bean Salad (page 69).

SPICED BEEF STEW
with Sweet Potatoes

MAKES: 8 servings ▪ **HANDS-ON TIME:** 50 min. ▪ **TOTAL TIME:** 6 hours, 50 min.

1   (6-oz.) can tomato paste
1   (32-oz.) container beef broth
1   (3-lb.) boneless chuck roast,
      trimmed and cut into
      1½-inch cubes
3   Tbsp. all-purpose flour
1½ tsp. table salt
1   tsp. freshly ground black pepper
2   Tbsp. olive oil
2   lb. small sweet potatoes,
      peeled and cubed
2   sweet onions, cut into eighths
4   garlic cloves, minced
2   celery ribs, sliced
2   cups cubed butternut squash
      (about 1 lb.)
2   cups frozen whole kernel corn,
      thawed
2   tsp. ancho chile powder
1   tsp. smoked paprika
1   tsp. dried thyme
Herbed Biscuits

1. Whisk together first 2 ingredients until smooth.
2. Sprinkle beef with flour, salt, and black pepper; toss to coat.
3. Cook beef, in batches, in hot oil in a large skillet over medium-high heat, stirring occasionally, 10 to 12 minutes or until browned. Place in a 6-qt. slow cooker. Add sweet potatoes, next 8 ingredients, and broth mixture. Cover and cook on HIGH 6 to 7 hours or until tender. Serve with Herbed Biscuits.

Herbed Biscuits

MAKES: 15 biscuits ▪ **HANDS-ON TIME:** 15 min. ▪ **TOTAL TIME:** 30 min.

½   cup cold butter, cubed
2   cups self-rising flour
2   Tbsp. fresh chives, chopped
2   Tbsp. fresh basil, chopped
1   tsp. freshly ground black pepper
1   cup buttermilk
Parchment paper

Preheat oven to 425°. Cut butter into flour with a pastry blender or fork until crumbly. Add chives, basil, and black pepper. Add buttermilk, stirring just until dry ingredients are moistened. Turn dough out onto a lightly floured surface, and knead lightly 3 or 4 times. Pat or roll dough to ¾-inch thickness; cut into squares to form 15 biscuits. Place on a parchment paper-lined baking sheet. Bake at 425° for 15 minutes or until golden.

ROASTED SWEET POTATO SALAD

MAKES: 4 to 6 servings ▪ **HANDS-ON TIME:** 20 min. ▪ **TOTAL TIME:** 1 hour, 5 min.

1 (24-oz.) package fresh steam-in-bag petite sweet potatoes
1 Tbsp. Caribbean jerk seasoning
4 Tbsp. olive oil, divided
2 Tbsp. fresh lime juice
1/4 tsp. table salt
1 (5-oz.) package baby arugula
1 mango, peeled and diced
1 avocado, halved and thinly sliced
1/2 red bell pepper, sliced
1/2 small red onion, sliced
1/2 cup torn fresh basil

1. Preheat oven to 425°. Cut potatoes in half lengthwise; toss with jerk seasoning and 1 Tbsp. oil. Arrange, cut sides down, in a single layer on a lightly greased baking sheet. Bake 15 minutes; turn and bake 8 to 10 more minutes or until tender. Cool on a wire rack 20 minutes.

2. Whisk together lime juice, salt, and remaining 3 Tbsp. oil in a large bowl. Add arugula and next 5 ingredients, and toss to coat. Arrange on a platter; top with potatoes.

Mango, avocado, red bell pepper, and sweet potatoes make a colorful presentation as well as a good-for-you meal.

TURKEY SALAD
with Cranberry Dressing

MAKES: 8 servings ▪ HANDS-ON TIME: 20 min. ▪ TOTAL TIME: 35 min.

2   Tbsp. butter, melted
½   tsp. dried Italian seasoning
4   medium-size dinner rolls, cut
      into 2-inch cubes (about 2 cups)
1   (5.5-oz.) package spring
      greens mix
1   small head romaine lettuce,
      chopped
2   cups coarsely chopped turkey
      or ham
½   English cucumber, thinly sliced
½   cup balsamic vinegar
2   garlic cloves, minced
½   cup canola oil
¼   cup whole-berry cranberry
      sauce
2   Tbsp. Dijon mustard
¼   tsp. table salt
¼   tsp. black pepper

1. Preheat oven to 425°. Stir together first 2 ingredients in a bowl. Add bread cubes; toss to coat. Bake cubes in a single layer in a jelly-roll pan 3 to 5 minutes or until golden, stirring once. Cool completely on a wire rack (about 15 minutes).

2. Combine spring greens, next 3 ingredients, and toasted bread cubes in a serving bowl. Process vinegar and next 6 ingredients in a blender until smooth. Serve with salad.

HAM WALDORF SALAD
pictured on page 251

MAKES: about 6 cups ▪ HANDS-ON TIME: 10 min. ▪ TOTAL TIME: 10 min.

3   cups chopped cooked ham
1   cup seedless red grapes, halved
1   large Gala apple, diced
1   cup diced celery
½   cup chopped toasted walnuts
½   cup mayonnaise
2   Tbsp. chopped fresh flat-leaf
      parsley
3   Tbsp. honey mustard
2   green onions, chopped
Mini pita halves
Fresh arugula

Stir together ham, grapes, apple, celery, walnuts, mayonnaise, parsley, honey mustard, green onions, and salt and pepper to taste in a large bowl. Serve in mini pita halves with fresh arugula.

OPEN-FACED SWEET POTATO-MUSHROOM SANDWICHES

MAKES: 6 sandwiches ▪ **HANDS-ON TIME:** 10 min. ▪ **TOTAL TIME:** 10 min.

1   cup mashed cooked sweet
        potatoes
3   oz. goat cheese, crumbled
½   tsp. ground chipotle chile pepper
12   (3-inch) square rye bread slices,
        toasted
3   thick bacon slices
½   cup sliced sweet onion
Fresh sliced shiitake mushrooms
        (5 large)
½   tsp. chopped fresh thyme
Fresh thyme sprigs

1. Preheat oven to 425°. Stir together potatoes and next 2 ingredients. Spread mixture onto bread slices.
2. Cook bacon slices in a skillet over medium heat 4 to 5 minutes or until crisp; remove bacon. Drain on paper towels, reserving 1 Tbsp. drippings in skillet. Crumble bacon.
3. Sauté onion in hot drippings until caramelized. Add mushrooms and ½ tsp. thyme; sauté 2 minutes. Stir in bacon; spoon over sweet potato mixture.
4. Place sandwiches on a baking sheet. Bake at 425° for 8 minutes. Top with fresh thyme sprigs.

GREEN BEAN CASSEROLE SANDWICH

MAKES: 1 sandwich ▪ **HANDS-ON TIME:** 10 min. ▪ **TOTAL TIME:** 10 min.

Butter
2   small pumpernickel party rye
        bread slices
Green bean casserole
1   shaved Parmesan cheese slice

1. Spread butter on 1 side of bread slices. Place 1 slice, buttered side down, on wax paper; top with 1 heaping Tbsp. green bean casserole and 1 shaved Parmesan cheese slice. Top with remaining bread slice, buttered side up.
2. Cook in a nonstick skillet over medium heat 2 to 3 minutes on each side or until golden brown and cheese melts.

OPEN-FACED SWEET
POTATO-MUSHROOM
SANDWICHES

GREEN BEAN
CASSEROLE SANDWICH

HAM WALDORF SALAD
PAGE 249

TURKEY-SPINACH WRAPS
PAGE 253

SMOKED TURKEY-BLUE
CHEESE OPEN-FACED
SANDWICHES

SMOKED TURKEY-BLUE CHEESE OPEN-FACED SANDWICHES

MAKES: 1 dozen ▪ **HANDS-ON TIME:** 10 min. ▪ **TOTAL TIME:** 10 min.

Fig paste
12 (¼-inch-thick) ciabatta or French bread slices, toasted
12 (1-oz.) slices roasted turkey
12 oz. soft ripened Brie
Parchment paper
Garnish: fresh arugula leaves

Preheat oven to 425°. Spread desired amount of fig paste on bread slices; top with turkey and Brie. Place on a parchment paper-lined baking sheet. Bake at 425° for 8 minutes. Remove from oven. Add pepper to taste.

Note: *We tested with Saga Soft-Ripened Blue-Veined cheese.*

TURKEY-SPINACH WRAPS
with Cranberry-Walnut-Cream Cheese Spread

MAKES: about 3 dozen ▪ **HANDS-ON TIME:** 30 min. ▪ **TOTAL TIME:** 30 min.

1 (8-oz.) package cream cheese, softened
2 (4-oz.) packages goat cheese, softened
¾ cup sweetened dried cranberries, coarsely chopped
¼ cup chopped toasted walnuts
2 tsp. honey
1 garlic clove, minced
½ tsp. chopped fresh rosemary
¼ tsp. black pepper
8 (10-inch) burrito-size flour tortillas
1 lb. thinly sliced cooked turkey
1 (6-oz.) package fresh baby spinach

Stir together first 8 ingredients. Add salt to taste. Cover and chill up to 3 days. Spread 2 Tbsp. cream cheese mixture onto each tortilla, leaving a ½-inch border around edges. Divide turkey and spinach among tortillas. Roll up, and cut in half or into slices.

Make Ahead: *Make these sandwiches up to 3 days in advance. They're perfect for a light Christmas supper or lunch when the holidays are over.*

PANCETTA-ARUGULA-TURKEY SANDWICHES

Not a fan of blue cheese? Try soft Brie instead.

MAKES: 6 servings ▪ **HANDS-ON TIME:** 15 min. ▪ **TOTAL TIME:** 15 min.

12   multigrain sourdough bakery
      bread slices
5   oz. soft ripened blue cheese
1½   lb. sliced roasted turkey
½   cup whole-berry cranberry
      sauce
6   cooked pancetta slices
2   cups loosely packed arugula
¼   cup whole grain Dijon mustard

Spread 1 side of 6 bread slices with blue cheese. Layer with turkey and next 3 ingredients. Spread 1 side of remaining 6 bread slices with mustard, and place, mustard sides down, on arugula.

Note: *We tested with Saga Soft-Ripened Blue-Veined Cheese.*

Try this twist!

Bacon-Horseradish Turkey Sandwiches: Substitute 6 split croissants for bread, 6 Havarti cheese slices for blue cheese, 6 cooked bacon slices for pancetta, and peach preserves for cranberry sauce. Stir 1 Tbsp. refrigerated horseradish into peach preserves. Proceed as directed.

TURKEY-BRIE-APPLE PANINI

MAKES: 4 servings ▪ **HANDS-ON TIME:** 20 min. ▪ **TOTAL TIME:** 1 hour, 15 min., including marmalade

1   (7-oz.) Brie round
1   medium-size Gala apple
8   Italian bread slices
1   cup loosely packed arugula
½   lb. thinly sliced smoked turkey
Bacon Marmalade
1   Tbsp. butter, melted

1. Preheat panini press. Trim and discard rind from Brie; cut into ¼-inch-thick slices. Cut apple into slices. Layer 4 bread slices with Brie, apple, arugula, and turkey. Top each with 1 bread slice spread with 1 Tbsp. Bacon Marmalade. Brush sandwiches with melted butter.
2. Cook sandwiches, in batches, in panini press 3 to 4 minutes or until golden brown and cheese melts. Serve immediately.

Bacon Marmalade

Try this on toast with a triple-cream cheese, tossed with iceberg lettuce and blue cheese, or spooned over ice cream.

MAKES: 1¼ cups ▪ **HANDS-ON TIME:** 25 min. ▪ **TOTAL TIME:** 55 min.

½   (16-oz.) package thick hickory-
       smoked bacon slices, diced
1   cup sorghum syrup
1½ cups apple cider vinegar
½   cup chicken broth
1   bay leaf

Cook bacon in a skillet over medium-high heat, stirring often, 4 minutes or until just dark golden brown; drain on paper towels. Wipe skillet clean; return bacon to skillet. Add sorghum; cook, stirring constantly, 1 minute. Add vinegar; cook, stirring often, 8 minutes or until liquid is reduced by half. Add broth and bay leaf; cook 5 minutes or until slightly thickened. Add kosher salt and freshly ground pepper to taste. Cool 30 minutes; remove and discard bay leaf.

CRANBERRY-TURKEY PANINI

MAKES: 6 servings ▪ **HANDS-ON TIME:** 15 min. ▪ **TOTAL TIME:** 23 min.

4   Tbsp. mayonnaise
4   Tbsp. horseradish Dijon mustard
4   soft sandwich rolls, cut in half
8   (1-oz.) Swiss or provolone
      cheese slices
8   (1-oz.) slices roasted turkey
1   cup cranberry sauce
Vegetable cooking spray

1. Preheat panini press. Spread mayonnaise and mustard on cut sides of rolls. Layer each bottom roll half with 1 cheese slice, and top evenly with turkey, cranberry, and remaining cheese slices. Cover with roll tops; spray tops with cooking spray.

2. Cook in panini press 2 to 3 minutes or until golden brown.

If you don't have a panini press, place the sandwiches in a hot skillet, and press with a smaller heavy pan. Cook until bread is golden brown; turn and continue cooking until the other side is golden brown and the cheese melts.

COUNTRY HAM-AND-PEACH PANINI

MAKES: 4 servings ▪ **HANDS-ON TIME:** 20 min. ▪ **TOTAL TIME:** 20 min.

8   ciabatta bread slices*
4   tsp. coarse-grained Dijon
      mustard
4   (1-oz.) fontina cheese slices
4   oz. thinly sliced country ham,
      prosciutto, or Serrano ham
2   medium-size peaches (about
      ¾ lb.), unpeeled and sliced
4   tsp. honey (optional)
1   Tbsp. extra virgin olive oil

1. Preheat panini press. Spread each of 4 bread slices with 1 tsp. mustard. Add black pepper to taste. Layer with cheese, ham, peaches, and, if desired, 1 tsp. honey. Top with remaining bread slices, and press together gently. Brush sandwiches with oil.

2. Cook sandwiches, in batches, in panini press 3 to 4 minutes or until golden brown and cheese melts. Serve immediately.

Any firm white bread may be substituted.

It's best to use very thinly sliced ham, not thick ham steaks. Ask the deli staff to slice it, or look for a packet of center- and end-cut slices, which tend to be smaller.

ROASTED SWEET POTATO-AND-ONION TART

MAKES: 6 to 8 servings ▪ **HANDS-ON TIME:** 30 min. ▪ **TOTAL TIME:** 2 hours, 40 min.

3 cups (¾-inch-cubed) sweet potatoes (about 1½ lb.)
1 cup chopped red onion
2 Tbsp. olive oil
1 tsp. seasoned pepper
6 cooked bacon slices, crumbled
¼ cup chopped fresh flat-leaf parsley
1 (14.1-oz.) package refrigerated piecrusts
2 cups (8 oz.) shredded Gruyère cheese
1½ cups half-and-half
4 large eggs
1 tsp. chopped fresh rosemary
½ tsp. table salt
Garnish: fresh rosemary

1. Preheat oven to 425°. Toss together first 4 ingredients in a large bowl; arrange mixture in a single layer in a lightly greased 15- x 10-inch jelly-roll pan. Bake at 425° for 20 minutes or just until potatoes are tender, stirring after 10 minutes. Cool completely in pan on a wire rack (about 30 minutes). Stir in bacon and parsley.

2. Unroll piecrusts; stack on a lightly greased surface. Roll stacked piecrusts into a 12-inch circle. Fit piecrust into a 10-inch deep-dish tart pan with removable bottom; press into fluted edges. Trim off excess piecrust along edges. Line piecrust with aluminum foil or parchment paper, and fill with pie weights or dried beans. Place pan on a foil-lined baking sheet.

3. Bake at 425° for 12 minutes. Remove weights and foil, and bake 5 more minutes. Cool completely on baking sheet on a wire rack (about 15 minutes). Reduce oven temperature to 350°.

4. Layer half of sweet potato mixture and half of cheese in tart shell; repeat layers once.

5. Whisk together half-and-half and next 3 ingredients; pour over cheese.

6. Bake at 350° on lowest oven rack 35 to 40 minutes or until set. Cool tart on baking sheet on a wire rack 15 minutes.

TURKEY CLUB
PIZZA

APPLE-GOAT
CHEESE PIZZA

MEXICAN PIZZA

SHRIMP-PESTO PIZZA

DAY-AFTER PIZZA

We used leftovers and extra ingredients for these pizzas.

MAKES: 6 servings ▪ **HANDS-ON TIME:** 20 min. ▪ **TOTAL TIME:** 40 min.

1   (11-oz.) can refrigerated thin
      pizza crust dough
Desired toppings

1. Preheat oven to 450°. Unroll dough; pat to an even thickness on a lightly greased baking sheet. Bake 10 to 12 minutes or until lightly browned.

2. Top and bake as directed in recipes below.

Try these twists!

Turkey Club Pizza: Stir together ¼ cup mayonnaise and 3 Tbsp. refrigerated reduced-fat pesto sauce; spread over crust. Top with 2 cups cubed cooked turkey, 2 thinly sliced plum tomatoes, and ¼ cup thinly sliced red onion. Bake at 450° for 6 to 8 minutes. Sprinkle with 1½ cups (6 oz.) shredded colby-Jack cheese and 4 cooked and crumbled bacon slices. Bake until cheese melts. Top with chopped fresh avocado.

Mexican Pizza: Sauté ½ lb. sliced smoked chorizo sausage and ½ cup thinly sliced sweet onion in 2 tsp. hot olive oil until onion is tender; drain. Combine 4 oz. softened cream cheese, 1 cup (4 oz.) shredded Monterey Jack cheese, ¼ cup chopped fresh cilantro, ½ tsp. lime zest, and 1 Tbsp. lime juice; spread over crust. Top with sausage mixture and 1½ cups fresh corn kernels. Bake at 450° for 8 to 10 minutes. Sprinkle with fresh cilantro leaves.

Apple-Goat Cheese Pizza: Sauté 1 thinly sliced Granny Smith apple and ½ cup thinly sliced red onion in 2 tsp. hot olive oil in a nonstick skillet until tender. Spread ⅓ cup fig preserves over crust. Top with apple mixture and 4 oz. crumbled goat cheese. Bake at 450° for 8 to 10 minutes or until cheese melts slightly. Top with 1 cup arugula and ½ cup chopped toasted pecans.

Shrimp-Pesto Pizza: Spread 3 Tbsp. refrigerated pesto sauce over crust. Top crust with ½ lb. peeled and cooked, medium-size shrimp and 1 cup halved grape tomatoes. Bake at 450° for 8 to 10 minutes. Sprinkle with ⅓ cup freshly grated Parmesan cheese and ¼ cup chopped fresh basil.

GREEN BEAN LASAGNA

MAKES: 8 servings • **HANDS-ON TIME:** 50 min. • **TOTAL TIME:** 2 hours, 25 min., including sauce

2 (14.4-oz.) packages frozen French-cut green beans, thawed

12 uncooked lasagna noodles

¼ cup butter, divided

2 large sweet onions, halved and sliced

8 oz. assorted fresh mushrooms, trimmed and sliced

¼ cup white wine

1 (15-oz.) container ricotta cheese

5 cups (20 oz.) shredded Italian cheese blend, divided

Parmesan Cream Sauce

1½ cups crushed round buttery crackers

1 (6-oz.) container French fried onions

3 Tbsp. butter, melted

1. Preheat oven to 350°. Drain green beans; pat dry with paper towels. Prepare noodles according to package directions.

2. Meanwhile, melt 2 Tbsp. butter in a large skillet over medium-high heat; add onions, and sauté 15 minutes or until golden brown. Transfer onions to a large bowl, and wipe skillet clean.

3. Melt remaining 2 Tbsp. butter in skillet; add fresh mushrooms, and sauté 4 to 5 minutes or until tender. Add wine, and sauté 3 minutes or until liquid is absorbed. Add mushrooms and green beans to caramelized onions in bowl; toss.

4. Stir together ricotta cheese and 1 cup shredded Italian cheese blend.

5. Layer 1 cup Parmesan Cream Sauce, 3 noodles, half of green bean mixture, and 1 cup cheese blend in a lightly greased 15- x 10-inch baking dish. Top with 1 cup Parmesan Cream Sauce, 3 noodles, and all of ricotta cheese mixture. Top with 3 noodles, remaining green bean mixture, 1 cup cheese blend, and 1 cup Parmesan Cream Sauce. Top sauce with remaining 3 noodles, 1 cup Parmesan Cream Sauce, and 2 cups cheese blend.

6. Bake at 350° for 50 minutes or until bubbly and golden brown. Toss together crackers and next 2 ingredients. Remove lasagna from oven; sprinkle cracker mixture over top. Bake 10 more minutes. Let stand on a wire rack 20 minutes before serving.

Parmesan Cream Sauce

MAKES: 4 cups • **HANDS-ON TIME:** 15 min. • **TOTAL TIME:** 15 min.

½ cup butter

⅓ cup all-purpose flour

4 cups milk

½ cup Parmesan cheese

¼ tsp. table salt

¼ tsp. freshly ground black pepper

Melt butter in a 3-qt. saucepan over medium-high heat. Whisk in flour, and cook, whisking constantly, 1 minute. Gradually whisk in milk; bring to a boil, and cook, whisking constantly, 1 to 2 minutes or until thickened. Whisk in Parmesan cheese, salt, and black pepper.

DINNER MAC-AND-CHEESE

Make a hearty mac-and-cheese by adding your leftover ham, veggies, and even crackers.

MAKES: 8 servings ▪ **HANDS-ON TIME:** 30 min. ▪ **TOTAL TIME:** 1 hour

1   (16-oz.) package uncooked cellentani (corkscrew) pasta
3   Tbsp. butter
¼   cup all-purpose flour
4   cups milk
1   cup (4 oz.) shredded sharp Cheddar cheese
1   (10-oz.) block sharp white Cheddar cheese, shredded
1   (3-oz.) package cream cheese, softened
½   tsp. table salt
2   cups chopped cooked ham
2   cups coarsely chopped assorted roasted vegetables
1¼ cups crushed round buttery crackers
2   Tbsp. butter, melted

1. Preheat oven to 400°. Prepare pasta according to package directions.

2. Meanwhile, melt 3 Tbsp. butter in a Dutch oven over medium heat. Gradually whisk in flour; cook, whisking constantly, 1 minute. Gradually whisk in milk until smooth; cook, whisking constantly, 8 to 10 minutes or until slightly thickened. Whisk in 1 cup sharp Cheddar cheese and next 3 ingredients until smooth. Remove from heat, and stir in ham, vegetables, and hot cooked pasta.

3. Spoon pasta mixture into a lightly greased 13- x 9-inch baking dish. Stir together crushed cracker crumbs and 2 Tbsp. melted butter; sprinkle over pasta mixture.

4. Bake at 400° for 25 to 30 minutes or until golden and bubbly. Let stand 5 minutes before serving.

"JEFFERSON" VIRGINIA HAM PASTA

This recipe is our nod to the Virginia wine country and Thomas Jefferson's love of pasta.

MAKES: 6 to 8 servings ▪ **HANDS-ON TIME:** 30 min. ▪ **TOTAL TIME:** 30 min.

2   (8.8-oz.) packages strozzapreti
     pasta
¼   lb. country ham, cut into ⅛-inch-
     thick strips (about ¾ cup)
2   Tbsp. olive oil
3   shallots, thinly sliced
8   oz. assorted wild mushrooms,
     sliced
1   garlic clove, thinly sliced
1   cup Viognier or dry white wine
½   cup frozen sweet peas
⅓   cup coarsely chopped fresh
     flat-leaf parsley
¼   cup heavy cream
3   Tbsp. butter
¼   tsp. pepper
1   cup freshly grated pecorino
     Romano cheese

1. Prepare pasta according to package directions.

2. Meanwhile, sauté ham in hot oil in a large skillet over medium heat 2 minutes or until lightly browned and crisp. Add shallots; sauté 1 minute. Add mushrooms and garlic, and cook, stirring often, 2 minutes or until mushrooms are tender. Stir in wine, and cook 5 minutes or until reduced by half.

3. Add peas, next 4 ingredients, and ½ cup cheese, stirring until cheese begins to melt and cream begins to thicken. Stir in hot cooked pasta, and toss until coated. Serve immediately with remaining ½ cup cheese.

CHICKEN AND CORNBREAD DUMPLINGS

MAKES: 8 servings ■ **HANDS-ON TIME:** 30 min. ■ **TOTAL TIME:** 5 hours, 40 min.

CHICKEN

3 skinned, bone-in chicken breasts
  (about 1½ lb.)
6 skinned and boned chicken
  thighs (about 1 lb.)
1 tsp. table salt
½ tsp. freshly ground black pepper
½ tsp. poultry seasoning
½ lb. carrots, sliced
½ lb. parsnips, sliced
4 celery ribs, sliced
1 sweet onion, chopped
2 (10¾-oz.) cans cream of
  chicken soup
1 (32-oz.) container chicken broth

CORNBREAD DUMPLINGS

1½ cups all-purpose flour
½ cup self-rising yellow
  cornmeal mix
2 tsp. baking powder
½ tsp. table salt
1 cup milk
3 Tbsp. butter, melted
¼ tsp. dried thyme
2 tsp. chopped fresh flat-leaf
  parsley

1. Prepare Chicken: Rub chicken pieces with salt, black pepper, and poultry seasoning. Place breasts in a 6-qt. slow cooker; top with thighs. Add carrots and next 3 ingredients. Whisk together soup and broth until smooth. Pour soup mixture over vegetables. Cover and cook on HIGH 3½ hours or until chicken shreds easily with a fork. Remove chicken; cool 10 minutes. Bone and shred chicken. Stir chicken into soup-and-vegetable mixture. Cover and cook on HIGH 1 hour or until boiling.

2. Prepare Dumplings: Whisk together flour and next 3 ingredients. Make a well in center of mixture. Add milk and next 3 ingredients to dry ingredients, gently stirring just until moistened.

3. Drop dough by ¼ cupfuls into simmering chicken mixture, leaving about ¼-inch space between dumplings. Cover and cook on HIGH 30 to 35 minutes or until dumplings have doubled in size.

HAM-AND-VEGETABLE COBBLER

MAKES: 6 servings ▪ HANDS-ON TIME: 30 min. ▪ TOTAL TIME: 1 hour, 10 min.

¼ cup butter
¼ cup all-purpose flour
3½ cups milk
1 tsp. chicken bouillon granules
½ tsp. dried thyme
2 cups diced cooked ham
1 (10-oz.) package frozen sweet peas and mushrooms
1 cup frozen crinkle-cut carrots
1 (14.1-oz.) package refrigerated piecrusts

1. Preheat oven to 450°. Melt butter in a large saucepan over medium heat. Gradually whisk in flour, and cook, whisking constantly, 1 minute. Add milk and next 2 ingredients; cook, stirring constantly, 6 to 8 minutes or until thickened and bubbly. Stir in ham and next 2 ingredients; cook 4 to 5 minutes or until mixture is thoroughly heated. Spoon into a lightly greased 11- x 7-inch baking dish.

2. Unroll each piecrust on a lightly floured surface. Cut piecrusts into 1¼-inch-wide strips. Arrange strips in a lattice design over ham mixture.

3. Bake at 450° for 40 minutes or until crust is browned and filling is bubbly.

NEXT-DAY TURKEY BAKE

MAKES: 6 servings ▪ HANDS-ON TIME: 15 min. ▪ TOTAL TIME: 1 hour, 35 min.

2½ cups coarsely chopped cooked turkey
2½ cups prepared cornbread dressing
1½ cups prepared turkey gravy, chilled
3 cups prepared mashed potatoes
1 Tbsp. butter

1. Preheat oven to 325°. Layer turkey, dressing, and gravy in a lightly greased 8-inch square baking dish. Spread mashed potatoes evenly over gravy, sealing edges. Dot evenly with butter.

2. Bake at 325° for 1 hour and 15 minutes. Let casserole stand 5 minutes before serving.

If the mashed potatoes won't spread, warm them slightly in the microwave with a little milk. After the big meal, large amounts of leftovers, such as cornbread dressing, should be divided into smaller portions (2 to 4 servings) so that they'll chill more quickly in the fridge.

HAM-AND-VEGETABLE COBBLER

12
Cocktails of Christmas

Distinguish your gatherings with beverages inspired by the season and crafted by experts from across the South

Hot Buttered Rye

1

2

3

4

CAPITAL EGGNOG

MAKES: 9 cups
HANDS-ON TIME: 35 min.
TOTAL TIME: 4 hours, 5 min.

Cook 6 cups milk, 2 cups heavy cream, and ⅛ tsp. ground nutmeg in a saucepan over medium heat, stirring occasionally, 5 to 7 minutes or until steaming (about 150°). Reduce heat to low. Whisk together 12 pasteurized egg yolks and 2 cups sugar in a large saucepan until smooth. Cook over low heat, whisking constantly, until mixture reaches at least 160° (about 25 minutes). Whisk milk mixture into egg mixture. Cool 30 minutes; transfer to a pitcher. Cover and chill 3 to 24 hours. Pour desired amount of praline or bourbon liqueur into each glass, if desired. Top with eggnog. Sprinkle with freshly ground nutmeg.

RECIPE FROM DAVID BURNETTE,
BARTENDER
THE CAPITAL HOTEL
LITTLE ROCK, ARKANSAS

HOT BUTTERED RYE

MAKES: 1 serving (and enough cream mixture for 6 drinks)
HANDS-ON TIME: 5 min.
TOTAL TIME: 1 hour, 10 min.

Beat 1 cup heavy cream and 2 Tbsp. maple syrup with an electric mixer at medium speed 2 minutes or until consistency of softened butter. Cover and chill 1 to 24 hours. Pour ¼ cup rye whiskey, 6 Tbsp. hot water, and 2 Tbsp. ginger liqueur into a 6-oz. heatproof cup. Top with about ¼ cup maple-cream mixture and freshly grated nutmeg.

RECIPE FROM STACIE STEWART,
BAR MANAGER
HARVEST
LOUISVILLE, KENTUCKY

ORANGE-CRANBERRY GIN AND TONIC

MAKES: 1 serving
HANDS-ON TIME: 5 min.
TOTAL TIME: 5 min.

Muddle 1 (2-inch) orange rind strip, 1 Tbsp. fresh cranberries,* and 1 tsp. sugar in a cocktail shaker. Add 1 cup ice cubes, 3 Tbsp. gin, and 1 Tbsp. fresh orange juice. Cover with lid, and shake vigorously until thoroughly chilled (about 30 seconds). Pour into an 8-oz. glass; top with ¼ cup tonic water. Serve immediately.

Frozen cranberries, thawed, may be substituted.

RECIPE FROM NORMAN KING,
OUR RESIDENT *SOUTHERN LIVING*
MIXOLOGIST

GINGERBREAD MARTINI

MAKES: 1 serving
HANDS-ON TIME: 5 min.
TOTAL TIME: 5 min.

Dip glass rims in ginger liqueur and crushed gingersnaps. Store glasses in freezer up to 2 days. Stir together 2 Tbsp. ginger liqueur, 2 Tbsp. vanilla-citrus liqueur, 1½ Tbsp. coffee-flavored rum, 1 Tbsp. honey, and 2 tsp. whipping cream in a cocktail shaker. Add 1 cup ice cubes; cover with lid, and shake vigorously until thoroughly chilled (about 30 seconds). Strain into a chilled martini glass. Garnish with a partially split vanilla bean brushed with liqueur and rolled in sugar, if desired.

Note: *We tested with Brinley Gold Coffee Rum, Tuaca Vanilla Citrus Liqueur, and Domaine de Canton ginger liqueur.*

RECIPE FROM KEN MACIEJEWSKI,
BAR MANAGER
TRISTAN
CHARLESTON, SOUTH CAROLINA

BAR LINGO

MUDDLE
Press ingredients, such as berries, herbs, and sugar, against the bottom and sides of a cocktail shaker using a muddler or back of a wooden spoon to release flavors.

⑤

MERRY BERRY CHRISTMAS, SUGAR!

MAKES: 1 serving
HANDS-ON TIME: 5 min.
TOTAL TIME: 5 min.

Muddle 5 fresh raspberries, 4 fresh blueberries, 2 fresh blackberries, 1½ Tbsp. light agave nectar, 5 fresh mint leaves, and 2 Tbsp. fresh lime juice in a cocktail shaker. Stir in 1 cup crushed ice and 6 Tbsp. water. Cover with lid, and shake vigorously until thoroughly chilled (7 to 10 seconds). Pour mixture into a 16-oz. glass, and top with 2 Tbsp. ginger ale. Garnish with halved fresh raspberries and blackberries, if desired.

RECIPE FROM RAMSEY PIMENTEL, LEAD MIXOLOGIST
THE RITZ-CARLTON, SOUTH BEACH
MIAMI, FLORIDA

⑥

SPARKLING CHARLESTON COSMO

MAKES: 1 serving
HANDS-ON TIME: 5 min.
TOTAL TIME: 5 min.

Combine 1 cup crushed ice, 3 Tbsp. vodka, 1½ Tbsp. peach nectar, 1 Tbsp. orange liqueur, and 1 Tbsp. white cranberry juice in a cocktail shaker. Squeeze juice from 2 lemon wedges into shaker. Place wedges in shaker. Cover with lid; shake vigorously until thoroughly chilled (about 30 seconds). Strain into a 6- to 8-oz. glass; discard lemon wedges and ice. Top with 2 Tbsp. sparkling white wine. Garnish with an orange slice, if desired.

Note: *We tested with Absolut Vodka.*

RECIPE FROM KEN MACIEJEWSKI, BAR MANAGER
TRISTAN
CHARLESTON, SOUTH CAROLINA

⑦

APPLE-ALE WASSAIL

MAKES: about 7 cups
HANDS-ON TIME: 5 min.
TOTAL TIME: 3 hours, 5 min.

Stir together 2 (12-oz.) bottles ale; 2 cups apple cider; 1 cup port; 1 cup lemonade; ¾ cup firmly packed light brown sugar; 1 apple, diced; 2 whole allspice; 2 (3-inch) cinnamon sticks; 6 whole cloves; and ⅛ tsp. ground cardamom in a 5-qt. slow cooker. Cover and cook on LOW 3 hours or until hot. Remove diced apple, if desired. Ladle into mugs. Garnish with lemon wedges and cinnamon sticks, if desired.

Note: *We tested with Sierra Nevada Tumbler Autumn Brown Ale.*

RECIPE FROM LARA CREASY, BEVERAGE DIRECTOR
JCT. KITCHEN & BAR AND NO. 246
ATLANTA, GEORGIA

⑧

PEAR-BASIL SIPPER

MAKES: 1 serving
HANDS-ON TIME: 5 min.
TOTAL TIME: 5 min.

Muddle 3 fresh basil leaves and ½ tsp. sugar in a cocktail shaker. Add 1 cup crushed ice, 4 Tbsp. pear nectar, and 3 Tbsp. pear-flavored vodka. Cover with lid, and shake vigorously until thoroughly chilled (about 30 seconds). Pour into a glass, and top with 3 Tbsp. lemon-lime soft drink. Garnish with a fresh basil sprig and a pear slice, if desired.

RECIPE FROM NORMAN KING, OUR RESIDENT *SOUTHERN LIVING* MIXOLOGIST

BAR LINGO

SHAKEN, NOT STIRRED Shaking ingredients with ice in a cocktail shaker makes the drink much colder than if stirred. Keep shaking until your hand is ice-cold and frost forms on the outside of the cocktail shaker.

---

(9)

PECAN "MILK" PUNCH

MAKES: about 2 cups
HANDS-ON TIME: 15 min.
TOTAL TIME: 3 hours, 33 min.

Bake 1 cup chopped pecans in a single layer in a shallow pan at 350° for 8 to 10 minutes or until toasted and fragrant, stirring once. Cool 10 minutes. Process pecans, ½ cup cane syrup, 1 Tbsp. cream of coconut, 1 tsp. ground cinnamon, ½ tsp. vanilla extract, and ⅛ tsp. kosher salt in a food processor 30 to 60 seconds or until smooth. With processor running, pour 1 cup water through food chute. Press mixture through a fine wire-mesh strainer into a pitcher, using back of spoon. Discard solids. Cover and chill 3 to 24 hours. Stir in ¼ cup bourbon just before serving. Serve over ice. Garnish with sweetened whipped cream and fresh mint leaves, if desired.

RECIPE FROM DREW STEVENS, GENERAL MANAGER SNACKBAR OXFORD, MISSISSIPPI

---

(10)

MISSISSIPPI BOURBON PUNCH

MAKES: about 14 cups
HANDS-ON TIME: 10 min.
TOTAL TIME: 10 min.

Pour 2 (750-milliliter) bottles dry muscadine wine, chilled;* 1 (12-oz.) bottle grenadine, chilled; 1½ cups chilled bourbon; 1 cup chilled fresh orange juice; 1 cup chilled cranberry juice; and ⅓ cup fresh lime juice into a punch bowl. Stir in 8 cups ice cubes; 1 (12-oz.) can lemon-lime soft drink, chilled; and 1 cup chilled club soda. Garnish with orange slices and red and green muscadine halves, if desired.

Chardonnay may be substituted.

Note: We tested with Morgan Creek Vineyards Cahaba White Alabama Muscadine wine and Stirrings grenadine.

RECIPE FROM JAYCE MCCONNELL, HEAD BARTENDER SNACKBAR OXFORD, MISSISSIPPI

---

(11)

VANILLA-ROSEMARY LEMONADE

MAKES: 6 cups
HANDS-ON TIME: 40 min.
TOTAL TIME: 4 hours, 10 min.

This is exceptional when made with freshly squeezed lemon juice.

Combine 1½ cups sugar; 1 vanilla bean, split; 3 small fresh rosemary sprigs; and 3 cups water in a medium saucepan. Bring to a light boil over medium heat, stirring occasionally. Simmer 5 minutes. Remove from heat, and let cool 30 minutes. Pour through a fine wire-mesh strainer into a large pitcher, discarding solids. Stir in 3 cups fresh lemon juice (about 26 to 30 lemons).* Cover and chill 3 to 48 hours. Stir just before serving over ice. Garnish with fresh rosemary sprigs and lemon slices, if desired.

3 (7.5-oz.) containers frozen lemon juice, thawed, may be substituted.

RECIPE FROM MAUREEN HOLT, CHEF AND CO-OWNER LITTLE SAVANNAH RESTAURANT BIRMINGHAM, ALABAMA

---

(12)

CHERRY FROST

MAKES: 1 serving
HANDS-ON TIME: 5 min.
TOTAL TIME: 5 min.

Combine 3 Tbsp. black cherry liqueur, 1 Tbsp. brandy, and 1 cup crushed ice in a cocktail shaker. Cover with lid, and shake vigorously until thoroughly chilled (about 30 seconds). Strain into a Champagne flute, and top with 4 Tbsp. sparkling white wine. Garnish with maraschino cherries, if desired.

Note: *We tested with Heering cherry liqueur and Riondo Prosecco Spago Nero.*

RECIPE FROM NORMAN KING, OUR RESIDENT *SOUTHERN LIVING* MIXOLOGIST

Menu Index

APPETIZER BUFFET
SERVES 8 TO 12

Roquefort Cheesecake
    with Pear Preserves and
    Pecans (page 30)
Hot Spinach-Artichoke Dip
    (page 30)
Tortellini Caprese Bites
    (page 34)
Mushroom Puffs (page 45)
Bacon-Wrapped Shrimp
    (page 46)
Mini Crab Cakes (page 53)

**COZY CHRISTMAS
DINNER**
SERVES 10 TO 12

Cheese Ring with Strawberry
    Preserves (page 33)
Creamy Chicken-and-Wild
    Rice Casserole (page 106)
Herbs and Greens Salad
    (Double Recipe) (page 66)
Icebox Dinner Rolls
    (page 188)
Red Velvet Cupcakes
    (page 152)

**TREE TRIMMING
SUPPER**
SERVES 6 TO 8

Roquefort Noodles
    (page 102)
Butternut Squash Soup
    (page 241)
Crusty French bread
Chocolate-Pecan Chess Pie
    (page 176)

**CONTINENTAL
CHRISTMAS EVE
BREAKFAST**
SERVES 6 TO 8

Cream Cheese-Filled
    Wreath (page 220)
Blueberry Muffins with
    Lemon-Cream Cheese
    Glaze (page 231)
Cornbread Biscuits
    (page 196)
Mustard-Peach Preserves
    (page 183)
Fresh fruit
Coffee and orange juice

METRIC EQUIVALENTS

The recipes that appear in this cookbook use the standard United States method
for measuring liquid and dry or solid ingredients (teaspoons, tablespoons, and cups).
The information in the following charts is provided to help cooks outside the U.S.
successfully use these recipes. All equivalents are approximate.

Metric Equivalents for Different Types of Ingredients

A standard cup measure of a dry or solid ingredient will vary in weight depending on the type of ingredient. A standard cup of liquid is the same volume for any type of liquid. Use the following chart when converting standard cup measures to grams (weight) or milliliters (volume).

Standard Cup	Fine Powder (ex. flour)	Grain (ex. rice)	Granular (ex. sugar)	Liquid Solids (ex. butter)	Liquid (ex. milk)
1	140 g	150 g	190 g	200 g	240 ml
¾	105 g	113 g	143 g	150 g	180 ml
⅔	93 g	100 g	125 g	133 g	160 ml
½	70 g	75 g	95 g	100 g	120 ml
⅓	47 g	50 g	63 g	67 g	80 ml
¼	35 g	38 g	48 g	50 g	60 ml
⅛	18 g	19 g	24 g	25 g	30 ml

Useful Equivalents for Dry Ingredients by Weight

(To convert ounces to grams, multiply the number of ounces by 30.)

1 oz	=	¹⁄₁₆ lb	=	30 g
4 oz	=	¼ lb	=	120 g
8 oz	=	½ lb	=	240 g
12 oz	=	¾ lb	=	360 g
16 oz	=	1 lb	=	480 g

Useful Equivalents for Length

(To convert inches to centimeters, multiply the number of inches by 2.5.)

1 in				=	2.5 cm	
6 in	=	½ ft		=	15 cm	
12 in	=	1 ft		=	30 cm	
36 in	=	3 ft	= 1 yd	=	90 cm	
40 in				=	100 cm	= 1 m

Useful Equivalents for Liquid Ingredients by Volume

¼ tsp						=	1 ml	
½ tsp						=	2 ml	
1 tsp						=	5 ml	
3 tsp	=	1 Tbsp			=	½ fl oz	=	15 ml
		2 Tbsp	=	⅛ cup	=	1 fl oz	=	30 ml
		4 Tbsp	=	¼ cup	=	2 fl oz	=	60 ml
		5⅓ Tbsp	=	⅓ cup	=	3 fl oz	=	80 ml
		8 Tbsp	=	½ cup	=	4 fl oz	=	120 ml
		10⅔ Tbsp	=	⅔ cup	=	5 fl oz	=	160 ml
		12 Tbsp	=	¾ cup	=	6 fl oz	=	180 ml
		16 Tbsp	=	1 cup	=	8 fl oz	=	240 ml
		1 pt	=	2 cups	=	16 fl oz	=	480 ml
		1 qt	=	4 cups	=	32 fl oz	=	960 ml
						33 fl oz	=	1000 ml = 1 l

Useful Equivalents for Cooking/Oven Temperatures

	Fahrenheit	Celsius	Gas Mark
Freeze water	32° F	0° C	
Room temperature	68° F	20° C	
Boil water	212° F	100° C	
Bake	325° F	160° C	3
	350° F	180° C	4
	375° F	190° C	5
	400° F	200° C	6
	425° F	220° C	7
	450° F	230° C	8
Broil			Grill

RECIPE INDEX

Hard Cover:
ISBN 13: 978-0-8487-3957-7
ISBN 10: 8487-3957-4
Library of Congress Control Number: 2013937131

Soft Cover:
ISBN 13: 978-0-8487-3956-0
ISBN 10: 8487-3956-6
Library of Congress Control Number: 2013937132

Printed in the United States of America
First Printing 2013

Oxmoor House

Editorial Director: Leah McLaughlin
Creative Director: Felicity Keane
Senior Brand Manager: Daniel Fagan
Senior Editor: Rebecca Brennan
Managing Editor: Rebecca Benton

Southern Living Best-Loved Christmas Classics

Editor: Susan Ray
Art Director: Claire Cormany
Assistant Designer: Allison Sperando Potter
Director, Test Kitchen: Elizabeth Tyler Austin
Assistant Directors, Test Kitchen: Julie Christopher,
    Julie Gunter
Recipe Developers and Testers: Wendy Ball, R.D.;
    Victoria E. Cox; Tamara Goldis; Stefanie Maloney;
    Callie Nash; Karen Rankin; Leah Van Deren
Recipe Editor: Alyson Moreland Haynes
Food Stylists: Margaret Monroe Dickey,
    Catherine Crowell Steele
Photography Director: Jim Bathie
Senior Photographer: Hélène Dujardin
Senior Photo Stylist: Kay E. Clarke
Photo Stylist: Mindi Shapiro Levine
Assistant Photo Stylist: Mary Louise Menendez
Senior Production Managers: Greg A. Amason,
    Susan Chodakiewicz

Contributors

Project Editor: Katie Strasser
Compositor: Frances Gunnells
Recipe Developers and Testers: Erica Hopper,
    Tonya Johnson, Kyra Moncrief, Kathleen Royal Phillips
Copy Editors: Susan Kemp, Norma E. McKittrick
Proofreaders: Adrienne Davis, Rhonda Lee Lother
Indexer: Mary Ann Laurens
Interns: Sara Lyon, Staley McIlwain, Jeffrey Preis,
    Maria Sanders, Julia Sayers
Photo Stylists: Caitlin Van Horn

Southern Living®

Editor: M. Lindsay Bierman
Creative Director: Robert Perino
Managing Editor: Candace Higginbotham
Art Director: Chris Hoke
Executive Editors: Rachel Hardage Barrett, Hunter Lewis,
    Jessica S. Thuston
Food Director: Shannon Sliter Satterwhite
Senior Food Editor: Mary Allen Perry
Deputy Food Director: Whitney Wright
Test Kitchen Director: Robby Melvin
Recipe Editor: JoAnn Weatherly
Assistant Recipe Editor: Ashley Arthur
Test Kitchen Specialist/Food Styling:
    Vanessa McNeil Rocchio
Test Kitchen Professionals: Norman King, Pam Lolley,
    Angela Sellers
Photographers: Robbie Caponetto, Laurey W. Glenn,
    Hector Sanchez
Senior Photo Stylist: Buffy Hargett
Editorial Assistant: Pat York

Time Home Entertainment Inc.

Publisher: Jim Childs
Vice President, Brand & Digital Strategy:
    Steven Sandonato
Executive Director, Marketing Services: Carol Pittard
Executive Director, Retail & Special Sales: Tom Mifsud
Director, Bookazine Development & Marketing:
    Laura Adam
Executive Publishing Director: Joy Butts
Associate Publishing Director: Megan Pearlman
Finance Director: Glenn Buonocore
Associate General Counsel: Helen Wan